my Sweet recipes

il mondo di ielle di Elena Pelizzoli

Volume n° ....

Dedicated to You
and your sweet world.

Love, ielle

il mondo di ielle
sugar Art
www.ilmondodiielle.com

Elena Pelizzoli©

My Sweet Recipes
Cakes and Desserts Recipe Book
50 Recipes

Copyright © 2018 Elena Pelizzoli

All rights reserved.
No part of this publication may be reproduced, stored in a retrieval system, or transmitted in any form or by any means, electronic, mechanical, photocopying, recording or otherwise, without the permission of the copyright holder.

I dedicate this book to
....

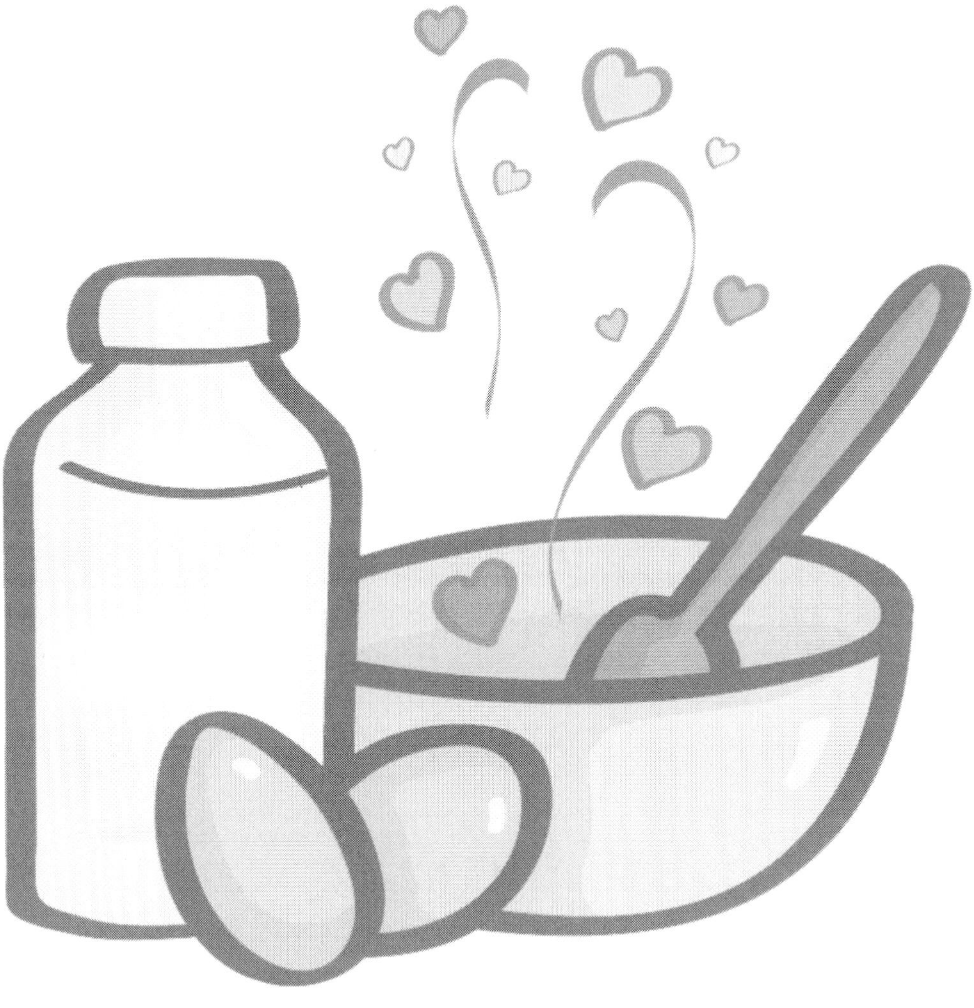

Summary

Recipe index
How to use this Recipe Book
Recipe Book
Notes
Weights and Measures
Bookmarks

Recipe index

N°	Recipe Name		Type of dessert	Difficulty	Rating
		Vol.			
		Vol.			
		Vol.			
		Vol.			
		Vol.			
		Vol.			
		Vol.			
		Vol.			
		Vol.			
		Vol.			
		Vol.			
		Vol.			
		Vol.			
		Vol.			
		Vol.			
		Vol.			
		Vol.			
		Vol.			
		Vol.			
		Vol.			

1 Recipe index

N°	Recipe Name	Type of dessert	Difficulty	Rating
	Vol.			
	Vol.			
	Vol.			
	Vol.			
	Vol.			
	Vol.			
	Vol.			
	Vol.			
	Vol.			
	Vol.			
	Vol.			
	Vol.			
	Vol.			
	Vol.			
	Vol.			
	Vol.			
	Vol.			
	Vol.			
	Vol.			
	Vol.			

Recipe index 2

N°	Recipe Name		Type of dessert	Difficulty	Rating
		Vol.		♙♙♙♙♙	☆☆☆☆☆
		Vol.		♙♙♙♙♙	☆☆☆☆☆
		Vol.		♙♙♙♙♙	☆☆☆☆☆
		Vol.		♙♙♙♙♙	☆☆☆☆☆
		Vol.		♙♙♙♙♙	☆☆☆☆☆
		Vol.		♙♙♙♙♙	☆☆☆☆☆
		Vol.		♙♙♙♙♙	☆☆☆☆☆
		Vol.		♙♙♙♙♙	☆☆☆☆☆
		Vol.		♙♙♙♙♙	☆☆☆☆☆
		Vol.		♙♙♙♙♙	☆☆☆☆☆
		Vol.		♙♙♙♙♙	☆☆☆☆☆
		Vol.		♙♙♙♙♙	☆☆☆☆☆
		Vol.		♙♙♙♙♙	☆☆☆☆☆
		Vol.		♙♙♙♙♙	☆☆☆☆☆
		Vol.		♙♙♙♙♙	☆☆☆☆☆
		Vol.		♙♙♙♙♙	☆☆☆☆☆
		Vol.		♙♙♙♙♙	☆☆☆☆☆
		Vol.		♙♙♙♙♙	☆☆☆☆☆
		Vol.		♙♙♙♙♙	☆☆☆☆☆
		Vol.		♙♙♙♙♙	☆☆☆☆☆

Recipe index

N°	Recipe Name	Type of dessert	Difficulty	Rating
	Vol.		♟♟♟♟	☆☆☆☆☆
	Vol.		♟♟♟♟	☆☆☆☆☆
	Vol.		♟♟♟♟	☆☆☆☆☆
	Vol.		♟♟♟♟	☆☆☆☆☆
	Vol.		♟♟♟♟	☆☆☆☆☆
	Vol.		♟♟♟♟	☆☆☆☆☆
	Vol.		♟♟♟♟	☆☆☆☆☆
	Vol.		♟♟♟♟	☆☆☆☆☆
	Vol.		♟♟♟♟	☆☆☆☆☆
	Vol.		♟♟♟♟	☆☆☆☆☆
	Vol.		♟♟♟♟	☆☆☆☆☆
	Vol.		♟♟♟♟	☆☆☆☆☆
	Vol.		♟♟♟♟	☆☆☆☆☆
	Vol.		♟♟♟♟	☆☆☆☆☆
	Vol.		♟♟♟♟	☆☆☆☆☆
	Vol.		♟♟♟♟	☆☆☆☆☆
	Vol.		♟♟♟♟	☆☆☆☆☆
	Vol.		♟♟♟♟	☆☆☆☆☆
	Vol.		♟♟♟♟	☆☆☆☆☆
	Vol.		♟♟♟♟	☆☆☆☆☆

Recipe index

N°	Recipe Name	🧁 Type of dessert	Difficulty	Rating
	Vol.		♙♙♙♙♙	☆☆☆☆☆
	Vol.		♙♙♙♙♙	☆☆☆☆☆
	Vol.		♙♙♙♙♙	☆☆☆☆☆
	Vol.		♙♙♙♙♙	☆☆☆☆☆
	Vol.		♙♙♙♙♙	☆☆☆☆☆
	Vol.		♙♙♙♙♙	☆☆☆☆☆
	Vol.		♙♙♙♙♙	☆☆☆☆☆
	Vol.		♙♙♙♙♙	☆☆☆☆☆
	Vol.		♙♙♙♙♙	☆☆☆☆☆
	Vol.		♙♙♙♙♙	☆☆☆☆☆
	Vol.		♙♙♙♙♙	☆☆☆☆☆
	Vol.		♙♙♙♙♙	☆☆☆☆☆
	Vol.		♙♙♙♙♙	☆☆☆☆☆
	Vol.		♙♙♙♙♙	☆☆☆☆☆
	Vol.		♙♙♙♙♙	☆☆☆☆☆
	Vol.		♙♙♙♙♙	☆☆☆☆☆
	Vol.		♙♙♙♙♙	☆☆☆☆☆
	Vol.		♙♙♙♙♙	☆☆☆☆☆
	Vol.		♙♙♙♙♙	☆☆☆☆☆
	Vol.		♙♙♙♙♙	☆☆☆☆☆

5 Recipe index

How to use this Recipe Book

How to use

IN THIS SPACE WRITE THE RECIPE NUMBER

WRITE HERE THE RECIPE NAME

MARKS THE LEVEL OF DIFFICULTY OF EXECUTION

CHOOSE THE LEVEL OF TASTINESS OF THE DESSERT

WRITE HERE THE DATE YOU WROTE THE RECIPE

WRITE HOW MANY SERVINGS YOU GET WITH THE QUANTITIES INDICATED

WRITE THE NAME OF THE AUTHOR OF THE RECIPE

HERE YOU CAN WRITE THE MEASUREMENTS, THE WEIGHT OF THE CAKE AND THE NUMBER OF PIECES OBTAINED WITH THE QUANTITIES INDICATED

Difficulty ♟♟♟♟♟ **Rating** ☆☆☆☆☆ **Date**

author

🏳 **Nationality**

🎂 **Dimensions** ⚖ **Weight** 🍰 **Pieces** 👥 **Serves**

WRITE THE NATIONALITY/ETHNICITY OF ORIGIN OF THE RECIPE

🧁 **Type** of dessert
- basic recipe
- cake
- chocolate
- cookie
- fried
- leavened
- pastry
- pie
- tart

CHOOSE OR WRITE DESSERT TYPE

Ingredients Quantity (Q) Percentage (I = Q.T×100) Cost

WRITE HERE THE LIST OF INGREDIENTS NECESSARY TO PREPARE THE DESSERT

WRITE THE AMOUNT OF EACH INGREDIENT. IF YOU WANT, YOU CAN ALSO CALCULATE THE PERCENTAGE AND THE COST. THE LAST COLUMN IS FREE, USE IT AS YOU WISH: YOU CAN PIN DIFFERENT QUANTITIES OR VARIATIONS, CALCULATE CALORIES, ETC.

DO YOU HAVE ALL THE INGREDIENTS? USE THIS SPACE TO CHECK THEM OFF THE LIST. ✓ USE A PENCIL SO YOU CAN DO IT SEVERAL TIMES

🎉 **Ideal for**
- breakfast
- dessert
- snacks
- occasion

CHOOSE AND/OR WRITE FOR WHICH OCCASION THIS DESSERT IS SUITABLE

TOTAL (Σ column values)
Per serving (TOTAL : Serves)

ADD THE VALUES OF EACH COLUMN TO FIND THE TOTAL QUANTITY AND COST. IF YOU WANT, YOU CAN CALCULATE THE QUANTITY, THE % AND THE COST OF A PORTION. THE LAST LINES ARE FREE.

❄ **Seasonal**
- spring
- summer
- fall
- winter
- year round

CHOOSE THE MOST SUITABLE SEASON TO PREPARE THE DESSERT CONSIDERING THE AVAILABILITY OF THE INGREDIENTS USED

🍴 **Utensils**
- baking dish
- baking paper
- baking tin
- baking tray
- blender
- bowl
- cake scraper
- chopping board
- cling film
- cookie cutter
- cooking pan
- cooling rack
- cup
- digital thermometer
- dough mixer
- electric whisk
- fork

- grater
- kitchen scissors
- kitchen torch
- knife
- ladle
- measuring cups set
- measuring spoons set
- mixer
- pastry brush
- piping bag
- piping nozzle
- pot
- potato peeler

- revolving cake stand
- rolling pin
- rubber spatula
- sieve
- skimmer
- saucepan
- spoon

✗ **Special diet**
- egg-free
- fat-free
- gluten-free
- lactose-free
- sugar-free
- vegan
- vegetarian

IF THIS DESSERT IS SUITABLE FOR A SPECIAL DIET YOU CAN IDICATE IT HERE

HERE YOU CAN CHECK OUT THE UTENSILS YOU NEED TO PREPARE THE DESSERT

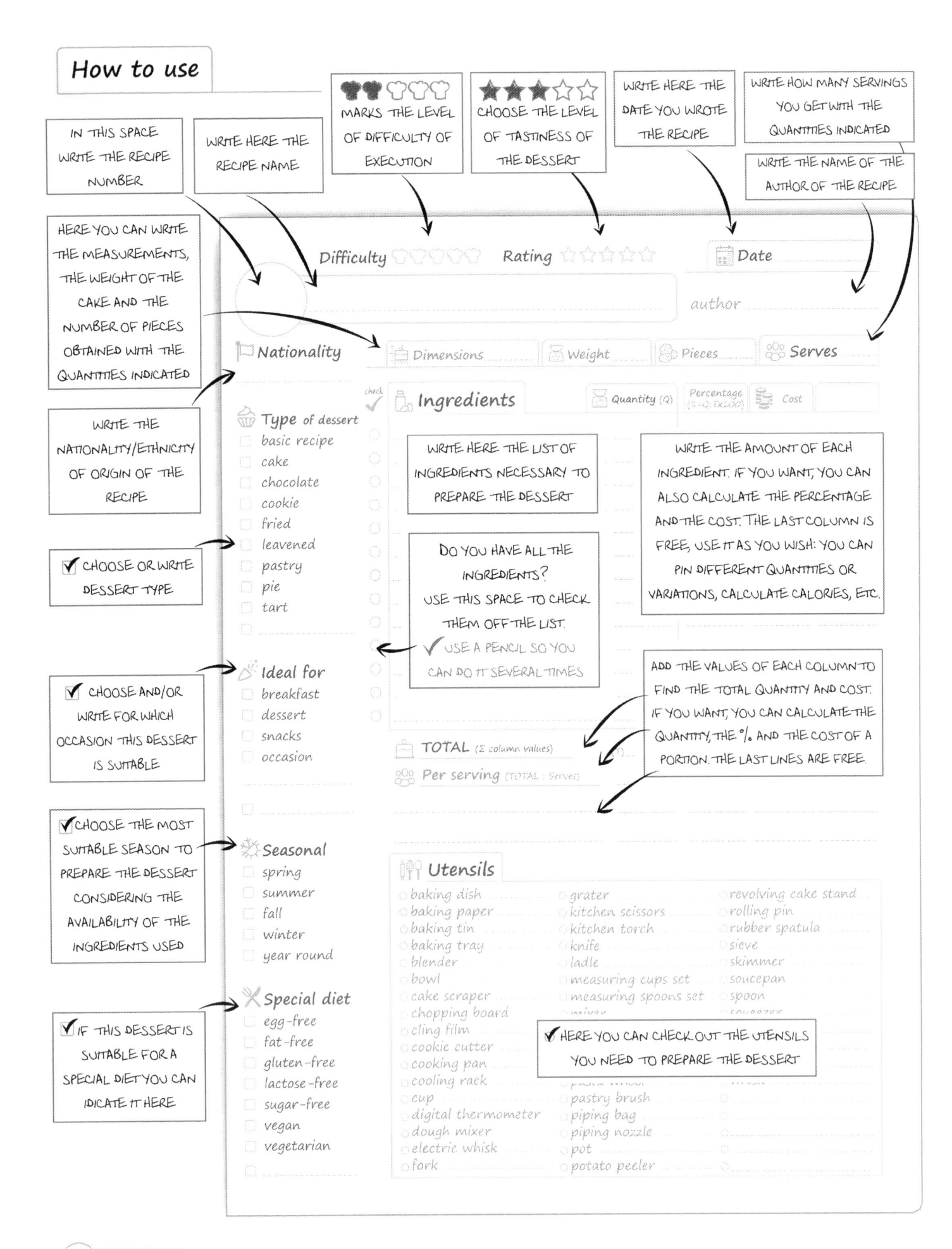

1 How to use

How to use

WRITE HERE ALL THE PROCEDURES NECESSARY TO PREPARE THE DESSERT

Instructions

Procedure / Time
- cooking
- cooling
- decorating
- freezing
- prepping
- proofing
- rest

TOT time

Cooking — temp. / time
- bain-marie
- cooktop
- fan oven
- fryer
- grill
- microwave
- static oven

Preservation — temp. / time
- freezer
- fridge
- room temp.

container
- airtight container
- cling film
- food-grade bag

Recipes used
- Vol.
- Vol.
- Vol.
- Vol.

Recipe's variants
- Vol.
- Vol.

Recipe

ARE THERE ANY TIPS, TRICKS, METHODS TO BE RESPECTED IN ORDER TO MAKE THE RECIPE PERFECT? TAKE NOTES HERE

Notes

Picture

YOU CAN USE THIS SPACE TO MAKE A DRAWING OR TO PASTE THE PHOTO OF THE DESSERT

Memo

DO YOU HAVE TO REMEMBER TO BUY MILK FOR THE RECIPE OR TO PREPARE THE DECORATIONS IN ADVANCE? TAKE NOTES HERE. USE A PENCIL SO YOU CAN USE IT SEVERAL TIMES

- ✓ CHOOSE AND/OR WRITE THE PROCEDURES AND THE TIME NECESSARY TO MAKE THE RECIPE
- ✓ CHOOSE AND/OR WRITE THE COOKING METHOD, TEMPERATURE AND TIME NEEDED
- ✓ CHOOSE AND/OR WRITE THE DESSERT PRESERVATION MODE, THE TEMPERATURE AND THE MAXIMUM TIME
- ✓ CHOOSE AND/OR WRITE THE CONTAINER TO USE TO PRESERVE THE DESSERT
- IF, TO MAKE THIS DESSERT, YOU USED RECIPES ALREADY WRITTEN, HERE YOU CAN INDICATE THE NUMBER, THE NAME AND THE VOLUME
- IF YOU HAVE VARIATIONS OF THIS RECIPE, YOU CAN WRITE THEM HERE
- WRITE THE RECIPE NUMBER

Recipe Book

This Recipe Book belongs to

....

Difficulty ♛♛♛♛♛ **Rating** ☆☆☆☆☆   📅 **Date** ....

.... *author* ....

🚩 **Nationality** .... | 🍰 Dimensions .... | ⚖️ Weight .... | 🍪 Pieces .... | 👥 Serves ....

🧁 **Type** of dessert
- ☐ basic recipe
- ☐ cake
- ☐ chocolate
- ☐ cookie
- ☐ fried
- ☐ leavened
- ☐ pastry
- ☐ pie
- ☐ tart
- ☐ ....

🎉 **Ideal for**
- ☐ breakfast
- ☐ dessert
- ☐ snacks
- ☐ occasion
- ☐ ....

❄️ **Seasonal**
- ☐ spring
- ☐ summer
- ☐ fall
- ☐ winter
- ☐ year round

🍴 **Special diet**
- ☐ egg-free
- ☐ fat-free
- ☐ gluten-free
- ☐ lactose-free
- ☐ sugar-free
- ☐ vegan
- ☐ vegetarian
- ☐ ....

check	🧂 Ingredients	⚖️ Quantity (Q)	Percentage (%=Q:T×100)	💰 Cost
○				
○				
○				
○				
○				
○				
○				
○				
○				
○				
○				
○				
○				
○				
○				

🍰 **TOTAL** (Σ column values) .... (T).......... 100%

👥 **Per serving** (TOTAL : Serves) ....

🍴 **Utensils**
- ○ baking dish
- ○ baking paper
- ○ baking tin
- ○ baking tray
- ○ blender
- ○ bowl
- ○ cake scraper
- ○ chopping board
- ○ cling film
- ○ cookie cutter
- ○ cooking pan
- ○ cooling rack
- ○ cup
- ○ digital thermometer
- ○ dough mixer
- ○ electric whisk
- ○ fork
- ○ grater
- ○ kitchen scissors
- ○ kitchen torch
- ○ knife
- ○ ladle
- ○ measuring cups set
- ○ measuring spoons set
- ○ mixer
- ○ mold
- ○ offset spatula
- ○ pasta roller
- ○ pasta wheel
- ○ pastry brush
- ○ piping bag
- ○ piping nozzle
- ○ pot
- ○ potato peeler
- ○ revolving cake stand
- ○ rolling pin
- ○ rubber spatula
- ○ sieve
- ○ skimmer
- ○ soucepan
- ○ spoon
- ○ squeezer
- ○ strainer
- ○ teaspoon
- ○ weight scale
- ○ whisk
- ○ ....
- ○ ....
- ○ ....
- ○ ....

Instructions

Notes

Picture

Memo

Procedure | Time
- [ ] cooking
- [ ] cooling
- [ ] decorating
- [ ] freezing
- [ ] prepping
- [ ] proofing
- [ ] rest
- [ ]

TOT time

Cooking | temp. | time
- [ ] bain-marie
- [ ] cooktop
- [ ] fan oven
- [ ] fryer
- [ ] grill
- [ ] microwave
- [ ] static oven
- [ ]

Preservation | temp. | time
- [ ] freezer
- [ ] fridge
- [ ] room temp.
- [ ]

container
- [ ] airtight container
- [ ] cling film
- [ ] food-grade bag
- [ ]

Recipes used
- Vol.
- Vol.
- Vol.
- Vol.

Recipe's variants
- Vol.
- Vol.

Recipe

Difficulty ♟♟♟♟♟ Rating ☆☆☆☆☆ 📅 Date ....

.... author ....

🚩 **Nationality** .... 🎂 Dimensions .... ⚖ Weight .... 🍪 Pieces .... 👥 Serves ....

check 📒 **Ingredients** ⚖ Quantity (Q) Percentage (%=Q:Tx100) 🪙 Cost

🧁 **Type** of dessert
- ☐ basic recipe
- ☐ cake
- ☐ chocolate
- ☐ cookie
- ☐ fried
- ☐ leavened
- ☐ pastry
- ☐ pie
- ☐ tart
- ☐ ....

🎉 **Ideal for**
- ☐ breakfast
- ☐ dessert
- ☐ snacks
- ☐ occasion

🎂 **TOTAL** (Σ column values) .... (T) .... 100% ....

👥 **Per serving** (TOTAL : Serves) ....

☐ ....

❄ **Seasonal**
- ☐ spring
- ☐ summer
- ☐ fall
- ☐ winter
- ☐ year round

🍴 **Utensils**

○ baking dish	○ grater	○ revolving cake stand
○ baking paper	○ kitchen scissors	○ rolling pin
○ baking tin	○ kitchen torch	○ rubber spatula
○ baking tray	○ knife	○ sieve
○ blender	○ ladle	○ skimmer
○ bowl	○ measuring cups set	○ soucepan
○ cake scraper	○ measuring spoons set	○ spoon
○ chopping board	○ mixer	○ squeezer
○ cling film	○ mold	○ strainer
○ cookie cutter	○ offset spatula	○ teaspoon
○ cooking pan	○ pasta roller	○ weight scale
○ cooling rack	○ pasta wheel	○ whisk
○ cup	○ pastry brush	○
○ digital thermometer	○ piping bag	○
○ dough mixer	○ piping nozzle	○
○ electric whisk	○ pot	○
○ fork	○ potato peeler	○

🍽 **Special diet**
- ☐ egg-free
- ☐ fat-free
- ☐ gluten-free
- ☐ lactose-free
- ☐ sugar-free
- ☐ vegan
- ☐ vegetarian
- ☐ ....

Instructions

Procedure   Time
- [ ] cooking
- [ ] cooling
- [ ] decorating
- [ ] freezing
- [ ] prepping
- [ ] proofing
- [ ] rest
- [ ]

TOT time

Cooking   temp.   time
- [ ] bain-marie
- [ ] cooktop
- [ ] fan oven
- [ ] fryer
- [ ] grill
- [ ] microwave
- [ ] static oven
- [ ]

Preservation   temp.   time
- [ ] freezer
- [ ] fridge
- [ ] room temp.
- [ ]

container
- [ ] airtight container
- [ ] cling film
- [ ] food-grade bag
- [ ]

Notes

Recipes used
- Vol.
- Vol.
- Vol.
- Vol.

Recipe's variants
- Vol.
- Vol.

Picture

Memo

Recipe

Difficulty ⌘⌘⌘⌘⌘ Rating ☆☆☆☆☆   📅 Date _____

_____   author _____

🚩 **Nationality** _____   🧂 Dimensions _____   ⚖ Weight _____   🍪 Pieces _____   👥 **Serves** _____

🧁 **Type** of dessert
- [ ] basic recipe
- [ ] cake
- [ ] chocolate
- [ ] cookie
- [ ] fried
- [ ] leavened
- [ ] pastry
- [ ] pie
- [ ] tart
- [ ] _____

🎉 **Ideal for**
- [ ] breakfast
- [ ] dessert
- [ ] snacks
- [ ] occasion
- [ ] _____

❄ **Seasonal**
- [ ] spring
- [ ] summer
- [ ] fall
- [ ] winter
- [ ] year round

🍴 **Special diet**
- [ ] egg-free
- [ ] fat-free
- [ ] gluten-free
- [ ] lactose-free
- [ ] sugar-free
- [ ] vegan
- [ ] vegetarian
- [ ] _____

check	🫙 **Ingredients**	⚖ Quantity (Q)	Percentage (%=Q:T×100)	🪙 Cost
○				
○				
○				
○				
○				
○				
○				
○				
○				
○				
○				
○				
○				
○				

🍰 **TOTAL** (Σ column values) _____ (T) _____ 100%

👥 **Per serving** (TOTAL : Serves) _____

🍴🥄 **Utensils**
- ○ baking dish
- ○ baking paper
- ○ baking tin
- ○ baking tray
- ○ blender
- ○ bowl
- ○ cake scraper
- ○ chopping board
- ○ cling film
- ○ cookie cutter
- ○ cooking pan
- ○ cooling rack
- ○ cup
- ○ digital thermometer
- ○ dough mixer
- ○ electric whisk
- ○ fork
- ○ grater
- ○ kitchen scissors
- ○ kitchen torch
- ○ knife
- ○ ladle
- ○ measuring cups set
- ○ measuring spoons set
- ○ mixer
- ○ mold
- ○ offset spatula
- ○ pasta roller
- ○ pasta wheel
- ○ pastry brush
- ○ piping bag
- ○ piping nozzle
- ○ pot
- ○ potato peeler
- ○ revolving cake stand
- ○ rolling pin
- ○ rubber spatula
- ○ sieve
- ○ skimmer
- ○ soucepan
- ○ spoon
- ○ squeezer
- ○ strainer
- ○ teaspoon
- ○ weight scale
- ○ whisk
- ○ _____
- ○ _____
- ○ _____

Instructions

Procedure ⏱ Time
- [ ] cooking
- [ ] cooling
- [ ] decorating
- [ ] freezing
- [ ] prepping
- [ ] proofing
- [ ] rest
- [ ]

TOT time

Cooking   temp. time
- [ ] bain-marie
- [ ] cooktop
- [ ] fan oven
- [ ] fryer
- [ ] grill
- [ ] microwave
- [ ] static oven
- [ ]

Preservation   temp. time
- [ ] freezer
- [ ] fridge
- [ ] room temp.
- [ ]

container
- [ ] airtight container
- [ ] cling film
- [ ] food-grade bag
- [ ]

Notes

Recipes used
- ◯ Vol.
- ◯ Vol.
- ◯ Vol.
- ◯ Vol.

Recipe's variants
- ◯ Vol.
- ◯ Vol.

Picture

Memo

Recipe

Difficulty ☐☐☐☐☐ **Rating** ☆☆☆☆☆ 🗓 **Date** _____

_____ *author* _____

🚩 **Nationality** _____ 📏 **Dimensions** _____ ⚖ **Weight** _____ 🍪 **Pieces** _____ 👥 **Serves** _____

🧁 **Type** of dessert
- ☐ basic recipe
- ☐ cake
- ☐ chocolate
- ☐ cookie
- ☐ fried
- ☐ leavened
- ☐ pastry
- ☐ pie
- ☐ tart
- ☐ _____

🎉 **Ideal for**
- ☐ breakfast
- ☐ dessert
- ☐ snacks
- ☐ occasion

☐ _____

❄ **Seasonal**
- ☐ spring
- ☐ summer
- ☐ fall
- ☐ winter
- ☐ year round

🍴 **Special diet**
- ☐ egg-free
- ☐ fat-free
- ☐ gluten-free
- ☐ lactose-free
- ☐ sugar-free
- ☐ vegan
- ☐ vegetarian
- ☐ _____

check ✓

🫙 **Ingredients** ⚖ **Quantity** (Q) **Percentage** (%=Q:T×100) 🪙 **Cost**

○ _____
○ _____
○ _____
○ _____
○ _____
○ _____
○ _____
○ _____
○ _____
○ _____
○ _____
○ _____
○ _____
○ _____
○ _____
○ _____
○ _____

🎂 **TOTAL** (Σ column values) (T) _____ 100% _____

👥 **Per serving** (TOTAL : Serves) _____

🍴 **Utensils**

○ baking dish	○ grater	○ revolving cake stand
○ baking paper	○ kitchen scissors	○ rolling pin
○ baking tin	○ kitchen torch	○ rubber spatula
○ baking tray	○ knife	○ sieve
○ blender	○ ladle	○ skimmer
○ bowl	○ measuring cups set	○ soucepan
○ cake scraper	○ measuring spoons set	○ spoon
○ chopping board	○ mixer	○ squeezer
○ cling film	○ mold	○ strainer
○ cookie cutter	○ offset spatula	○ teaspoon
○ cooking pan	○ pasta roller	○ weight scale
○ cooling rack	○ pasta wheel	○ whisk
○ cup	○ pastry brush	○
○ digital thermometer	○ piping bag	○
○ dough mixer	○ piping nozzle	○
○ electric whisk	○ pot	○
○ fork	○ potato peeler	○

Instructions

Procedure | Time
- [ ] cooking
- [ ] cooling
- [ ] decorating
- [ ] freezing
- [ ] prepping
- [ ] proofing
- [ ] rest
- [ ]

TOT time

Cooking | temp. | time
- [ ] bain-marie
- [ ] cooktop
- [ ] fan oven
- [ ] fryer
- [ ] grill
- [ ] microwave
- [ ] static oven
- [ ]

Preservation | temp. | time
- [ ] freezer
- [ ] fridge
- [ ] room temp.
- [ ]

container
- [ ] airtight container
- [ ] cling film
- [ ] food-grade bag
- [ ]

Notes

Recipes used
- ◯ _____ Vol.
- ◯ _____ Vol.
- ◯ _____ Vol.
- ◯ _____ Vol.

Recipe's variants
- ◯ _____ Vol.
- ◯ _____ Vol.

Recipe

Picture

Memo

Difficulty ☱☱☱☱☱ **Rating** ☆☆☆☆☆   📅 Date ....

....   author ....

🚩 Nationality .... 🎂 Dimensions .... ⚖ Weight .... 🍪 Pieces .... 👥 Serves ....

🧁 **Type** of dessert
- ☐ basic recipe
- ☐ cake
- ☐ chocolate
- ☐ cookie
- ☐ fried
- ☐ leavened
- ☐ pastry
- ☐ pie
- ☐ tart
- ☐ ....

🎉 **Ideal for**
- ☐ breakfast
- ☐ dessert
- ☐ snacks
- ☐ occasion

☐ ....

❄ **Seasonal**
- ☐ spring
- ☐ summer
- ☐ fall
- ☐ winter
- ☐ year round

🍴 **Special diet**
- ☐ egg-free
- ☐ fat-free
- ☐ gluten-free
- ☐ lactose-free
- ☐ sugar-free
- ☐ vegan
- ☐ vegetarian
- ☐ ....

check	🧴 Ingredients	⚖ Quantity (Q)	Percentage (%=Q:T×100)	💰 Cost
○				
○				
○				
○				
○				
○				
○				
○				
○				
○				
○				
○				
○				
○				

🎂 **TOTAL** (Σ column values) .... (T) .... 100% ....

👥 **Per serving** (TOTAL : Serves) ....

🍴 **Utensils**
- ○ baking dish
- ○ baking paper
- ○ baking tin
- ○ baking tray
- ○ blender
- ○ bowl
- ○ cake scraper
- ○ chopping board
- ○ cling film
- ○ cookie cutter
- ○ cooking pan
- ○ cooling rack
- ○ cup
- ○ digital thermometer
- ○ dough mixer
- ○ electric whisk
- ○ fork
- ○ grater
- ○ kitchen scissors
- ○ kitchen torch
- ○ knife
- ○ ladle
- ○ measuring cups set
- ○ measuring spoons set
- ○ mixer
- ○ mold
- ○ offset spatula
- ○ pasta roller
- ○ pasta wheel
- ○ pastry brush
- ○ piping bag
- ○ piping nozzle
- ○ pot
- ○ potato peeler
- ○ revolving cake stand
- ○ rolling pin
- ○ rubber spatula
- ○ sieve
- ○ skimmer
- ○ soucepan
- ○ spoon
- ○ squeezer
- ○ strainer
- ○ teaspoon
- ○ weight scale
- ○ whisk
- ○ ....
- ○ ....
- ○ ....

Instructions

Procedure | Time
- [ ] cooking
- [ ] cooling
- [ ] decorating
- [ ] freezing
- [ ] prepping
- [ ] proofing
- [ ] rest
- [ ]

TOT time

Cooking | temp. | time
- [ ] bain-marie
- [ ] cooktop
- [ ] fan oven
- [ ] fryer
- [ ] grill
- [ ] microwave
- [ ] static oven
- [ ]

Preservation | temp. | time
- [ ] freezer
- [ ] fridge
- [ ] room temp.
- [ ]

container
- [ ] airtight container
- [ ] cling film
- [ ] food-grade bag
- [ ]

Notes

Picture

Memo

Recipes used
- Vol.
- Vol.
- Vol.
- Vol.

Recipe's variants
- Vol.
- Vol.

Recipe

Difficulty ♛♛♛♛♛ **Rating** ☆☆☆☆☆ 📅 **Date** ....

.... *author* ....

🚩 **Nationality** .... 📦 **Dimensions** .... ⚖️ **Weight** .... 🍪 **Pieces** .... 👥 **Serves** ....

🧁 **Type** of dessert
- ☐ basic recipe
- ☐ cake
- ☐ chocolate
- ☐ cookie
- ☐ fried
- ☐ leavened
- ☐ pastry
- ☐ pie
- ☐ tart
- ☐ ....

🎉 **Ideal for**
- ☐ breakfast
- ☐ dessert
- ☐ snacks
- ☐ occasion

- ☐ ....

❄️ **Seasonal**
- ☐ spring
- ☐ summer
- ☐ fall
- ☐ winter
- ☐ year round

🍴 **Special diet**
- ☐ egg-free
- ☐ fat-free
- ☐ gluten-free
- ☐ lactose-free
- ☐ sugar-free
- ☐ vegan
- ☐ vegetarian
- ☐ ....

check	🍯 Ingredients	⚖️ Quantity (Q)	Percentage (%=Q:T×100)	🪙 Cost
○				
○				
○				
○				
○				
○				
○				
○				
○				
○				
○				
○				
○				
○				
○				

🎂 **TOTAL** (Σ column values) .... (T) 100%

👥 **Per serving** (TOTAL : Serves) ....

🍴 **Utensils**
- ○ baking dish
- ○ baking paper
- ○ baking tin
- ○ baking tray
- ○ blender
- ○ bowl
- ○ cake scraper
- ○ chopping board
- ○ cling film
- ○ cookie cutter
- ○ cooking pan
- ○ cooling rack
- ○ cup
- ○ digital thermometer
- ○ dough mixer
- ○ electric whisk
- ○ fork
- ○ grater
- ○ kitchen scissors
- ○ kitchen torch
- ○ knife
- ○ ladle
- ○ measuring cups set
- ○ measuring spoons set
- ○ mixer
- ○ mold
- ○ offset spatula
- ○ pasta roller
- ○ pasta wheel
- ○ pastry brush
- ○ piping bag
- ○ piping nozzle
- ○ pot
- ○ potato peeler
- ○ revolving cake stand
- ○ rolling pin
- ○ rubber spatula
- ○ sieve
- ○ skimmer
- ○ soucepan
- ○ spoon
- ○ squeezer
- ○ strainer
- ○ teaspoon
- ○ weight scale
- ○ whisk
- ○ ....
- ○ ....

Instructions

Procedure | Time
- [ ] cooking
- [ ] cooling
- [ ] decorating
- [ ] freezing
- [ ] prepping
- [ ] proofing
- [ ] rest
- [ ]

TOT time

Cooking | temp. | time
- [ ] bain-marie
- [ ] cooktop
- [ ] fan oven
- [ ] fryer
- [ ] grill
- [ ] microwave
- [ ] static oven
- [ ]

Preservation | temp. | time
- [ ] freezer
- [ ] fridge
- [ ] room temp.
- [ ]

container
- [ ] airtight container
- [ ] cling film
- [ ] food-grade bag
- [ ]

Notes

Recipes used
- Vol.
- Vol.
- Vol.
- Vol.

Recipe's variants
- Vol.
- Vol.

Picture

Memo

Recipe

Difficulty ♛♛♛♛♛   **Rating** ☆☆☆☆☆   📅 Date ....

....   author ....

🚩 Nationality ....   🍰 Dimensions ....   ⚖ Weight ....   🍪 Pieces ....   👥 Serves ....

🧁 **Type** of dessert
- ☐ basic recipe
- ☐ cake
- ☐ chocolate
- ☐ cookie
- ☐ fried
- ☐ leavened
- ☐ pastry
- ☐ pie
- ☐ tart
- ☐ ....

🎉 **Ideal for**
- ☐ breakfast
- ☐ dessert
- ☐ snacks
- ☐ occasion
- ☐ ....

❄ **Seasonal**
- ☐ spring
- ☐ summer
- ☐ fall
- ☐ winter
- ☐ year round

🍴 **Special diet**
- ☐ egg-free
- ☐ fat-free
- ☐ gluten-free
- ☐ lactose-free
- ☐ sugar-free
- ☐ vegan
- ☐ vegetarian
- ☐ ....

check	🧂 Ingredients	⚖ Quantity (Q)	Percentage (%=Q:T×100)	💰 Cost
○				
○				
○				
○				
○				
○				
○				
○				
○				
○				
○				
○				
○				
○				
○				

🍰 **TOTAL** (Σ column values) .... (T) .... 100% ....

👥 **Per serving** (TOTAL : Serves) ....

🍴 **Utensils**
- ○ baking dish
- ○ baking paper
- ○ baking tin
- ○ baking tray
- ○ blender
- ○ bowl
- ○ cake scraper
- ○ chopping board
- ○ cling film
- ○ cookie cutter
- ○ cooking pan
- ○ cooling rack
- ○ cup
- ○ digital thermometer
- ○ dough mixer
- ○ electric whisk
- ○ fork
- ○ grater
- ○ kitchen scissors
- ○ kitchen torch
- ○ knife
- ○ ladle
- ○ measuring cups set
- ○ measuring spoons set
- ○ mixer
- ○ mold
- ○ offset spatula
- ○ pasta roller
- ○ pasta wheel
- ○ pastry brush
- ○ piping bag
- ○ piping nozzle
- ○ pot
- ○ potato peeler
- ○ revolving cake stand
- ○ rolling pin
- ○ rubber spatula
- ○ sieve
- ○ skimmer
- ○ soucepan
- ○ spoon
- ○ squeezer
- ○ strainer
- ○ teaspoon
- ○ weight scale
- ○ whisk
- ○ ....
- ○ ....
- ○ ....

Instructions

Procedure | Time
- [ ] cooking
- [ ] cooling
- [ ] decorating
- [ ] freezing
- [ ] prepping
- [ ] proofing
- [ ] rest
- [ ]

TOT time

Cooking | temp. | time
- [ ] bain-marie
- [ ] cooktop
- [ ] fan oven
- [ ] fryer
- [ ] grill
- [ ] microwave
- [ ] static oven
- [ ]

Preservation | temp. | time
- [ ] freezer
- [ ] fridge
- [ ] room temp.
- [ ]

container
- [ ] airtight container
- [ ] cling film
- [ ] food-grade bag
- [ ]

Recipes used
- Vol.
- Vol.
- Vol.
- Vol.

Recipe's variants
- Vol.
- Vol.

Notes

Picture

Memo

Recipe

Difficulty ☆☆☆☆☆ **Rating** ☆☆☆☆☆   📅 **Date** ....

.... *author* ....

🚩 **Nationality** ....   🎂 **Dimensions** ....   ⚖️ **Weight** ....   🍪 **Pieces** ....   👥 **Serves** ....

🧁 **Type** of dessert
- [ ] basic recipe
- [ ] cake
- [ ] chocolate
- [ ] cookie
- [ ] fried
- [ ] leavened
- [ ] pastry
- [ ] pie
- [ ] tart
- [ ] ....

🎉 **Ideal for**
- [ ] breakfast
- [ ] dessert
- [ ] snacks
- [ ] occasion
- [ ] ....

❄️ **Seasonal**
- [ ] spring
- [ ] summer
- [ ] fall
- [ ] winter
- [ ] year round

🍴 **Special diet**
- [ ] egg-free
- [ ] fat-free
- [ ] gluten-free
- [ ] lactose-free
- [ ] sugar-free
- [ ] vegan
- [ ] vegetarian
- [ ] ....

check ✓

🫙 **Ingredients** | ⚖️ **Quantity** (Q) | **Percentage** (%=Q:T×100) | 🪙 **Cost**

(ingredient list — 17 blank rows)

🎂 **TOTAL** (Σ column values) .... (T) 100%

👥 **Per serving** (TOTAL : Serves) ....

🍴 **Utensils**

- ○ baking dish
- ○ baking paper
- ○ baking tin
- ○ baking tray
- ○ blender
- ○ bowl
- ○ cake scraper
- ○ chopping board
- ○ cling film
- ○ cookie cutter
- ○ cooking pan
- ○ cooling rack
- ○ cup
- ○ digital thermometer
- ○ dough mixer
- ○ electric whisk
- ○ fork
- ○ grater
- ○ kitchen scissors
- ○ kitchen torch
- ○ knife
- ○ ladle
- ○ measuring cups set
- ○ measuring spoons set
- ○ mixer
- ○ mold
- ○ offset spatula
- ○ pasta roller
- ○ pasta wheel
- ○ pastry brush
- ○ piping bag
- ○ piping nozzle
- ○ pot
- ○ potato peeler
- ○ revolving cake stand
- ○ rolling pin
- ○ rubber spatula
- ○ sieve
- ○ skimmer
- ○ soucepan
- ○ spoon
- ○ squeezer
- ○ strainer
- ○ teaspoon
- ○ weight scale
- ○ whisk
- ○ ....
- ○ ....
- ○ ....

Instructions

Procedure | Time
- [ ] cooking
- [ ] cooling
- [ ] decorating
- [ ] freezing
- [ ] prepping
- [ ] proofing
- [ ] rest
- [ ]

TOT time

Cooking | temp. | time
- [ ] bain-marie
- [ ] cooktop
- [ ] fan oven
- [ ] fryer
- [ ] grill
- [ ] microwave
- [ ] static oven
- [ ]

Preservation | temp. | time
- [ ] freezer
- [ ] fridge
- [ ] room temp.
- [ ]

container
- [ ] airtight container
- [ ] cling film
- [ ] food-grade bag
- [ ]

Recipes used
Vol.
Vol.
Vol.
Vol.

Recipe's variants
Vol.
Vol.

Notes

Picture

Memo

Recipe

Difficulty ☐☐☐☐☐ **Rating** ☆☆☆☆☆   📅 **Date** ....

.... *author* ....

🚩 **Nationality** .... 🎂 **Dimensions** .... ⚖ **Weight** .... 🍪 **Pieces** .... 👥 **Serves** ....

🧁 **Type** of dessert

- ☐ basic recipe
- ☐ cake
- ☐ chocolate
- ☐ cookie
- ☐ fried
- ☐ leavened
- ☐ pastry
- ☐ pie
- ☐ tart
- ☐ ....

🎉 **Ideal for**

- ☐ breakfast
- ☐ dessert
- ☐ snacks
- ☐ occasion
- ☐ ....

❄ **Seasonal**

- ☐ spring
- ☐ summer
- ☐ fall
- ☐ winter
- ☐ year round

🍴 **Special diet**

- ☐ egg-free
- ☐ fat-free
- ☐ gluten-free
- ☐ lactose-free
- ☐ sugar-free
- ☐ vegan
- ☐ vegetarian
- ☐ ....

check	🧂 **Ingredients**	⚖ Quantity (Q)	Percentage (%=Q:T×100)	🪙 Cost
○				
○				
○				
○				
○				
○				
○				
○				
○				
○				
○				
○				
○				
○				

🎂 **TOTAL** (Σ column values) .... (T) 100%

👥 **Per serving** (TOTAL : Serves) ....

🍴 **Utensils**

- ○ baking dish
- ○ baking paper
- ○ baking tin
- ○ baking tray
- ○ blender
- ○ bowl
- ○ cake scraper
- ○ chopping board
- ○ cling film
- ○ cookie cutter
- ○ cooking pan
- ○ cooling rack
- ○ cup
- ○ digital thermometer
- ○ dough mixer
- ○ electric whisk
- ○ fork
- ○ grater
- ○ kitchen scissors
- ○ kitchen torch
- ○ knife
- ○ ladle
- ○ measuring cups set
- ○ measuring spoons set
- ○ mixer
- ○ mold
- ○ offset spatula
- ○ pasta roller
- ○ pasta wheel
- ○ pastry brush
- ○ piping bag
- ○ piping nozzle
- ○ pot
- ○ potato peeler
- ○ revolving cake stand
- ○ rolling pin
- ○ rubber spatula
- ○ sieve
- ○ skimmer
- ○ soucepan
- ○ spoon
- ○ squeezer
- ○ strainer
- ○ teaspoon
- ○ weight scale
- ○ whisk
- ○ ....
- ○ ....
- ○ ....

Instructions

Procedure | Time
- [ ] cooking
- [ ] cooling
- [ ] decorating
- [ ] freezing
- [ ] prepping
- [ ] proofing
- [ ] rest
- [ ] ....

TOT time

Cooking | temp. | time
- [ ] bain-marie
- [ ] cooktop
- [ ] fan oven
- [ ] fryer
- [ ] grill
- [ ] microwave
- [ ] static oven
- [ ] ....

Preservation | temp. | time
- [ ] freezer
- [ ] fridge
- [ ] room temp.
- [ ] ....

container
- [ ] airtight container
- [ ] cling film
- [ ] food-grade bag
- [ ] ....

Notes

Recipes used
- .... Vol. ....
- .... Vol. ....
- .... Vol. ....
- .... Vol. ....

Recipe's variants
- .... Vol. ....
- .... Vol. ....

Picture

Memo

Recipe

Difficulty 🍪🍪🍪🍪🍪 **Rating** ☆☆☆☆☆ 📅 **Date** _____

_____

author _____

🚩 **Nationality** _____ 🧁 **Dimensions** _____ ⚖️ **Weight** _____ 🍪 **Pieces** _____ 👥 **Serves** _____

🧁 **Type** of dessert
- ☐ basic recipe
- ☐ cake
- ☐ chocolate
- ☐ cookie
- ☐ fried
- ☐ leavened
- ☐ pastry
- ☐ pie
- ☐ tart
- ☐ _____

🎉 **Ideal for**
- ☐ breakfast
- ☐ dessert
- ☐ snacks
- ☐ occasion
- ☐ _____

❄️ **Seasonal**
- ☐ spring
- ☐ summer
- ☐ fall
- ☐ winter
- ☐ year round

✗ **Special diet**
- ☐ egg-free
- ☐ fat-free
- ☐ gluten-free
- ☐ lactose-free
- ☐ sugar-free
- ☐ vegan
- ☐ vegetarian
- ☐ _____

check ✓ | 🍯 **Ingredients** | ⚖️ **Quantity** (Q) | **Percentage** (%=Q:T×100) | 🪙 **Cost**

(lined entries)

🎂 **TOTAL** (Σ column values) _____ (T) _____ 100% _____

👥 **Per serving** (TOTAL : Serves) _____

🍴 **Utensils**

○ baking dish	○ grater	○ revolving cake stand
○ baking paper	○ kitchen scissors	○ rolling pin
○ baking tin	○ kitchen torch	○ rubber spatula
○ baking tray	○ knife	○ sieve
○ blender	○ ladle	○ skimmer
○ bowl	○ measuring cups set	○ soucepan
○ cake scraper	○ measuring spoons set	○ spoon
○ chopping board	○ mixer	○ squeezer
○ cling film	○ mold	○ strainer
○ cookie cutter	○ offset spatula	○ teaspoon
○ cooking pan	○ pasta roller	○ weight scale
○ cooling rack	○ pasta wheel	○ whisk
○ cup	○ pastry brush	○
○ digital thermometer	○ piping bag	○
○ dough mixer	○ piping nozzle	○
○ electric whisk	○ pot	○
○ fork	○ potato peeler	○

Instructions

Procedure | Time
- [ ] cooking
- [ ] cooling
- [ ] decorating
- [ ] freezing
- [ ] prepping
- [ ] proofing
- [ ] rest
- [ ]

TOT time

Cooking | temp. | time
- [ ] bain-marie
- [ ] cooktop
- [ ] fan oven
- [ ] fryer
- [ ] grill
- [ ] microwave
- [ ] static oven
- [ ]

Preservation | temp. | time
- [ ] freezer
- [ ] fridge
- [ ] room temp.
- [ ]

container
- [ ] airtight container
- [ ] cling film
- [ ] food-grade bag
- [ ]

Recipes used
Vol.
Vol.
Vol.
Vol.

Recipe's variants
Vol.
Vol.

Recipe

Notes

Picture

Memo

Difficulty ♙♙♙♙♙ Rating ☆☆☆☆☆ 📅 Date ....

.... author ....

🚩 Nationality .... 📦 Dimensions .... ⚖ Weight .... 🍪 Pieces .... 👥 Serves ....

🧁 **Type** of dessert
- [ ] basic recipe
- [ ] cake
- [ ] chocolate
- [ ] cookie
- [ ] fried
- [ ] leavened
- [ ] pastry
- [ ] pie
- [ ] tart
- [ ] ....

🎉 **Ideal for**
- [ ] breakfast
- [ ] dessert
- [ ] snacks
- [ ] occasion

- [ ] ....

❄ **Seasonal**
- [ ] spring
- [ ] summer
- [ ] fall
- [ ] winter
- [ ] year round

🍴 **Special diet**
- [ ] egg-free
- [ ] fat-free
- [ ] gluten-free
- [ ] lactose-free
- [ ] sugar-free
- [ ] vegan
- [ ] vegetarian
- [ ] ....

check ✓ 🧂 **Ingredients** ⚖ Quantity (Q) Percentage (%=Q:T×100) 🪙 Cost

🎂 **TOTAL** (Σ column values) (T) 100%

👥 **Per serving** (TOTAL : Serves)

🍴 **Utensils**
- ○ baking dish
- ○ baking paper
- ○ baking tin
- ○ baking tray
- ○ blender
- ○ bowl
- ○ cake scraper
- ○ chopping board
- ○ cling film
- ○ cookie cutter
- ○ cooking pan
- ○ cooling rack
- ○ cup
- ○ digital thermometer
- ○ dough mixer
- ○ electric whisk
- ○ fork
- ○ grater
- ○ kitchen scissors
- ○ kitchen torch
- ○ knife
- ○ ladle
- ○ measuring cups set
- ○ measuring spoons set
- ○ mixer
- ○ mold
- ○ offset spatula
- ○ pasta roller
- ○ pasta wheel
- ○ pastry brush
- ○ piping bag
- ○ piping nozzle
- ○ pot
- ○ potato peeler
- ○ revolving cake stand
- ○ rolling pin
- ○ rubber spatula
- ○ sieve
- ○ skimmer
- ○ soucepan
- ○ spoon
- ○ squeezer
- ○ strainer
- ○ teaspoon
- ○ weight scale
- ○ whisk

Instructions

Procedure ⏱ Time
☐ cooking
☐ cooling
☐ decorating
☐ freezing
☐ prepping
☐ proofing
☐ rest
☐

TOT time

Cooking 🌡 temp. ⏱ time
☐ bain-marie
☐ cooktop
☐ fan oven
☐ fryer
☐ grill
☐ microwave
☐ static oven
☐

Preservation 🌡 temp. ⏱ time
☐ freezer
☐ fridge
☐ room temp.
☐

container
☐ airtight container
☐ cling film
☐ food-grade bag
☐

Notes

Recipes used
○ _____ Vol.
○ _____ Vol.
○ _____ Vol.
○ _____ Vol.

Recipe's variants
○ _____ Vol.
○ _____ Vol.

📷 Picture

Memo

Recipe

Difficulty ♙♙♙♙♙   Rating ☆☆☆☆☆   📅 Date ....

....   author ....

🚩 Nationality ....   📦 Dimensions ....   ⚖ Weight ....   🍪 Pieces ....   👥 Serves ....

🧁 **Type** of dessert
- ☐ basic recipe
- ☐ cake
- ☐ chocolate
- ☐ cookie
- ☐ fried
- ☐ leavened
- ☐ pastry
- ☐ pie
- ☐ tart
- ☐ ....

🎉 **Ideal for**
- ☐ breakfast
- ☐ dessert
- ☐ snacks
- ☐ occasion
- ☐ ....

❄ **Seasonal**
- ☐ spring
- ☐ summer
- ☐ fall
- ☐ winter
- ☐ year round

🍴 **Special diet**
- ☐ egg-free
- ☐ fat-free
- ☐ gluten-free
- ☐ lactose-free
- ☐ sugar-free
- ☐ vegan
- ☐ vegetarian
- ☐ ....

check	🥛 **Ingredients**	⚖ Quantity (Q)	Percentage (%=Q:T×100)	🪙 Cost
○	....	....	....	....
○	....	....	....	....
○	....	....	....	....
○	....	....	....	....
○	....	....	....	....
○	....	....	....	....
○	....	....	....	....
○	....	....	....	....
○	....	....	....	....
○	....	....	....	....
○	....	....	....	....
○	....	....	....	....

🎂 **TOTAL** (Σ column values) .... (T) 100%

👥 **Per serving** (TOTAL : Serves) ....

🍴 **Utensils**

- ○ baking dish
- ○ baking paper
- ○ baking tin
- ○ baking tray
- ○ blender
- ○ bowl
- ○ cake scraper
- ○ chopping board
- ○ cling film
- ○ cookie cutter
- ○ cooking pan
- ○ cooling rack
- ○ cup
- ○ digital thermometer
- ○ dough mixer
- ○ electric whisk
- ○ fork
- ○ grater
- ○ kitchen scissors
- ○ kitchen torch
- ○ knife
- ○ ladle
- ○ measuring cups set
- ○ measuring spoons set
- ○ mixer
- ○ mold
- ○ offset spatula
- ○ pasta roller
- ○ pasta wheel
- ○ pastry brush
- ○ piping bag
- ○ piping nozzle
- ○ pot
- ○ potato peeler
- ○ revolving cake stand
- ○ rolling pin
- ○ rubber spatula
- ○ sieve
- ○ skimmer
- ○ soucepan
- ○ spoon
- ○ squeezer
- ○ strainer
- ○ teaspoon
- ○ weight scale
- ○ whisk
- ○ ....
- ○ ....
- ○ ....

Instructions

Procedure | Time
- [ ] cooking
- [ ] cooling
- [ ] decorating
- [ ] freezing
- [ ] prepping
- [ ] proofing
- [ ] rest
- [ ]

TOT time

Cooking | temp. | time
- [ ] bain-marie
- [ ] cooktop
- [ ] fan oven
- [ ] fryer
- [ ] grill
- [ ] microwave
- [ ] static oven
- [ ]

Preservation | temp. | time
- [ ] freezer
- [ ] fridge
- [ ] room temp.
- [ ]

container
- [ ] airtight container
- [ ] cling film
- [ ] food-grade bag
- [ ]

Notes

Recipes used
- Vol.
- Vol.
- Vol.
- Vol.

Recipe's variants
- Vol.
- Vol.

Picture

Memo

Recipe

Difficulty ♟♟♟♟♟ Rating ☆☆☆☆☆   📅 Date ....

....   author ....

🚩 Nationality ....   📦 Dimensions .... ⚖️ Weight .... 🍪 Pieces .... 👥 Serves ....

🧁 Type of dessert
- [ ] basic recipe
- [ ] cake
- [ ] chocolate
- [ ] cookie
- [ ] fried
- [ ] leavened
- [ ] pastry
- [ ] pie
- [ ] tart
- [ ] ....

🎉 Ideal for
- [ ] breakfast
- [ ] dessert
- [ ] snacks
- [ ] occasion
- [ ] ....

❄️ Seasonal
- [ ] spring
- [ ] summer
- [ ] fall
- [ ] winter
- [ ] year round

🍴 Special diet
- [ ] egg-free
- [ ] fat-free
- [ ] gluten-free
- [ ] lactose-free
- [ ] sugar-free
- [ ] vegan
- [ ] vegetarian
- [ ] ....

check 🍯 Ingredients | Quantity (Q) | Percentage (%=Q:T×100) | 💰 Cost

TOTAL (Σ column values) .... (T) 100%

👥 **Per serving** (TOTAL : Serves) ....

🍴 Utensils
- ○ baking dish
- ○ baking paper
- ○ baking tin
- ○ baking tray
- ○ blender
- ○ bowl
- ○ cake scraper
- ○ chopping board
- ○ cling film
- ○ cookie cutter
- ○ cooking pan
- ○ cooling rack
- ○ cup
- ○ digital thermometer
- ○ dough mixer
- ○ electric whisk
- ○ fork
- ○ grater
- ○ kitchen scissors
- ○ kitchen torch
- ○ knife
- ○ ladle
- ○ measuring cups set
- ○ measuring spoons set
- ○ mixer
- ○ mold
- ○ offset spatula
- ○ pasta roller
- ○ pasta wheel
- ○ pastry brush
- ○ piping bag
- ○ piping nozzle
- ○ pot
- ○ potato peeler
- ○ revolving cake stand
- ○ rolling pin
- ○ rubber spatula
- ○ sieve
- ○ skimmer
- ○ soucepan
- ○ spoon
- ○ squeezer
- ○ strainer
- ○ teaspoon
- ○ weight scale
- ○ whisk

Instructions

Procedure | Time
- [ ] cooking
- [ ] cooling
- [ ] decorating
- [ ] freezing
- [ ] prepping
- [ ] proofing
- [ ] rest
- [ ]

TOT time

Cooking | temp. | time
- [ ] bain-marie
- [ ] cooktop
- [ ] fan oven
- [ ] fryer
- [ ] grill
- [ ] microwave
- [ ] static oven
- [ ]

Preservation | temp. | time
- [ ] freezer
- [ ] fridge
- [ ] room temp.
- [ ]

container
- [ ] airtight container
- [ ] cling film
- [ ] food-grade bag
- [ ]

Notes

Picture

Memo

Recipes used
- Vol.
- Vol.
- Vol.
- Vol.

Recipe's variants
- Vol.
- Vol.

Recipe

Difficulty 🎩🎩🎩🎩🎩   Rating ☆☆☆☆☆   📅 Date _____

author _____

🚩 **Nationality** _____   📦 Dimensions _____   ⚖️ Weight _____   🍪 Pieces _____   👥 **Serves** _____

🧁 Type of dessert
- ☐ basic recipe
- ☐ cake
- ☐ chocolate
- ☐ cookie
- ☐ fried
- ☐ leavened
- ☐ pastry
- ☐ pie
- ☐ tart
- ☐ _____

🎉 Ideal for
- ☐ breakfast
- ☐ dessert
- ☐ snacks
- ☐ occasion

- ☐ _____

❄️ Seasonal
- ☐ spring
- ☐ summer
- ☐ fall
- ☐ winter
- ☐ year round

🍴 Special diet
- ☐ egg-free
- ☐ fat-free
- ☐ gluten-free
- ☐ lactose-free
- ☐ sugar-free
- ☐ vegan
- ☐ vegetarian
- ☐ _____

check	🧂 **Ingredients**	⚖️ Quantity (Q)	Percentage (%=Q:T×100)	🪙 Cost
○				
○				
○				
○				
○				
○				
○				
○				
○				
○				
○				
○				
○				
○				
○				

🎂 **TOTAL** (Σ column values)   (T) _____   100%

👥 **Per serving** (TOTAL : Serves)

🍴 Utensils

- ○ baking dish
- ○ baking paper
- ○ baking tin
- ○ baking tray
- ○ blender
- ○ bowl
- ○ cake scraper
- ○ chopping board
- ○ cling film
- ○ cookie cutter
- ○ cooking pan
- ○ cooling rack
- ○ cup
- ○ digital thermometer
- ○ dough mixer
- ○ electric whisk
- ○ fork
- ○ grater
- ○ kitchen scissors
- ○ kitchen torch
- ○ knife
- ○ ladle
- ○ measuring cups set
- ○ measuring spoons set
- ○ mixer
- ○ mold
- ○ offset spatula
- ○ pasta roller
- ○ pasta wheel
- ○ pastry brush
- ○ piping bag
- ○ piping nozzle
- ○ pot
- ○ potato peeler
- ○ revolving cake stand
- ○ rolling pin
- ○ rubber spatula
- ○ sieve
- ○ skimmer
- ○ soucepan
- ○ spoon
- ○ squeezer
- ○ strainer
- ○ teaspoon
- ○ weight scale
- ○ whisk
- ○ _____
- ○ _____
- ○ _____

Instructions

Procedure | Time
- [ ] cooking
- [ ] cooling
- [ ] decorating
- [ ] freezing
- [ ] prepping
- [ ] proofing
- [ ] rest
- [ ] _____

TOT time

Cooking | temp. | time
- [ ] bain-marie
- [ ] cooktop
- [ ] fan oven
- [ ] fryer
- [ ] grill
- [ ] microwave
- [ ] static oven
- [ ] _____

Preservation | temp. | time
- [ ] freezer
- [ ] fridge
- [ ] room temp.
- [ ] _____

container
- [ ] airtight container
- [ ] cling film
- [ ] food-grade bag
- [ ] _____

Notes

Recipes used
- ○ _____ Vol.
- ○ _____ Vol.
- ○ _____ Vol.
- ○ _____ Vol.

Recipe's variants
- ○ _____ Vol.
- ○ _____ Vol.

Recipe

Picture

Memo

Difficulty 🎩🎩🎩🎩🎩 **Rating** ☆☆☆☆☆ **Date** ....

.... author ....

🚩 **Nationality** .... 📦 **Dimensions** .... ⚖ **Weight** .... 🍪 **Pieces** .... 👥 **Serves** ....

🧁 **Type** of dessert
- [ ] basic recipe
- [ ] cake
- [ ] chocolate
- [ ] cookie
- [ ] fried
- [ ] leavened
- [ ] pastry
- [ ] pie
- [ ] tart
- [ ] ....

🎉 **Ideal for**
- [ ] breakfast
- [ ] dessert
- [ ] snacks
- [ ] occasion
- [ ] ....

❄ **Seasonal**
- [ ] spring
- [ ] summer
- [ ] fall
- [ ] winter
- [ ] year round

🍴 **Special diet**
- [ ] egg-free
- [ ] fat-free
- [ ] gluten-free
- [ ] lactose-free
- [ ] sugar-free
- [ ] vegan
- [ ] vegetarian
- [ ] ....

check ✓ | 🥫 **Ingredients** | ⚖ **Quantity** (Q) | **Percentage** (%=Q:T×100) | 🪙 **Cost**

🎂 **TOTAL** (Σ column values) .... (T) .... 100% ....

👥 **Per serving** (TOTAL : Serves) ....

🍴 **Utensils**
- ○ baking dish
- ○ baking paper
- ○ baking tin
- ○ baking tray
- ○ blender
- ○ bowl
- ○ cake scraper
- ○ chopping board
- ○ cling film
- ○ cookie cutter
- ○ cooking pan
- ○ cooling rack
- ○ cup
- ○ digital thermometer
- ○ dough mixer
- ○ electric whisk
- ○ fork
- ○ grater
- ○ kitchen scissors
- ○ kitchen torch
- ○ knife
- ○ ladle
- ○ measuring cups set
- ○ measuring spoons set
- ○ mixer
- ○ mold
- ○ offset spatula
- ○ pasta roller
- ○ pasta wheel
- ○ pastry brush
- ○ piping bag
- ○ piping nozzle
- ○ pot
- ○ potato peeler
- ○ revolving cake stand
- ○ rolling pin
- ○ rubber spatula
- ○ sieve
- ○ skimmer
- ○ soucepan
- ○ spoon
- ○ squeezer
- ○ strainer
- ○ teaspoon
- ○ weight scale
- ○ whisk
- ○ ....
- ○ ....

Instructions

Procedure / Time
- [ ] cooking
- [ ] cooling
- [ ] decorating
- [ ] freezing
- [ ] prepping
- [ ] proofing
- [ ] rest
- [ ]

TOT time

Cooking — temp. / time
- [ ] bain-marie
- [ ] cooktop
- [ ] fan oven
- [ ] fryer
- [ ] grill
- [ ] microwave
- [ ] static oven
- [ ]

Preservation — temp. / time
- [ ] freezer
- [ ] fridge
- [ ] room temp.
- [ ]

container
- [ ] airtight container
- [ ] cling film
- [ ] food-grade bag
- [ ]

Notes

Picture

Memo

Recipes used
- Vol.
- Vol.
- Vol.
- Vol.

Recipe's variants
- Vol.
- Vol.

Recipe

Difficulty ♟♟♟♟♟ Rating ☆☆☆☆☆   📅 Date ....

....   author ....

🚩 Nationality .... 🎂 Dimensions .... ⚖ Weight .... 🍪 Pieces .... 👥 Serves ....

🧁 Type of dessert
- ☐ basic recipe
- ☐ cake
- ☐ chocolate
- ☐ cookie
- ☐ fried
- ☐ leavened
- ☐ pastry
- ☐ pie
- ☐ tart
- ☐ ....

🎉 Ideal for
- ☐ breakfast
- ☐ dessert
- ☐ snacks
- ☐ occasion
- ☐ ....

❄ Seasonal
- ☐ spring
- ☐ summer
- ☐ fall
- ☐ winter
- ☐ year round

🍴 Special diet
- ☐ egg-free
- ☐ fat-free
- ☐ gluten-free
- ☐ lactose-free
- ☐ sugar-free
- ☐ vegan
- ☐ vegetarian
- ☐ ....

check ✓ Ingredients   Quantity (Q)   Percentage (%=Q:T×100)   Cost

(ingredient lines)

🎂 TOTAL (Σ column values) .... (T) .... 100% ....

👥 Per serving (TOTAL : Serves) ....

🍴 Utensils

○ baking dish	○ grater	○ revolving cake stand
○ baking paper	○ kitchen scissors	○ rolling pin
○ baking tin	○ kitchen torch	○ rubber spatula
○ baking tray	○ knife	○ sieve
○ blender	○ ladle	○ skimmer
○ bowl	○ measuring cups set	○ soucepan
○ cake scraper	○ measuring spoons set	○ spoon
○ chopping board	○ mixer	○ squeezer
○ cling film	○ mold	○ strainer
○ cookie cutter	○ offset spatula	○ teaspoon
○ cooking pan	○ pasta roller	○ weight scale
○ cooling rack	○ pasta wheel	○ whisk
○ cup	○ pastry brush	○
○ digital thermometer	○ piping bag	○
○ dough mixer	○ piping nozzle	○
○ electric whisk	○ pot	○
○ fork	○ potato peeler	○

Instructions

Procedure | Time
- [ ] cooking
- [ ] cooling
- [ ] decorating
- [ ] freezing
- [ ] prepping
- [ ] proofing
- [ ] rest
- [ ]

TOT time

Cooking | temp. | time
- [ ] bain-marie
- [ ] cooktop
- [ ] fan oven
- [ ] fryer
- [ ] grill
- [ ] microwave
- [ ] static oven
- [ ]

Preservation | temp. | time
- [ ] freezer
- [ ] fridge
- [ ] room temp.
- [ ]

container
- [ ] airtight container
- [ ] cling film
- [ ] food-grade bag
- [ ]

Recipes used
- Vol.
- Vol.
- Vol.
- Vol.

Recipe's variants
- Vol.
- Vol.

Notes

Picture

Memo

Recipe

Difficulty ♧♧♧♧♧ **Rating** ☆☆☆☆☆ 📅 **Date** ____

_____ author ____

🚩 **Nationality** ____ 🎂 Dimensions ____ ⚖ Weight ____ 🍪 Pieces ____ 👥 **Serves** ____

check ✓ 🍯 **Ingredients**   ⚖ Quantity (Q)   Percentage (%=Q:T×100) 🪙 Cost

🧁 **Type** of dessert
- ☐ basic recipe
- ☐ cake
- ☐ chocolate
- ☐ cookie
- ☐ fried
- ☐ leavened
- ☐ pastry
- ☐ pie
- ☐ tart
- ☐ ____

🎉 **Ideal for**
- ☐ breakfast
- ☐ dessert
- ☐ snacks
- ☐ occasion

☐ ____

🎂 **TOTAL** (Σ column values) .... (T) 100%

👥 **Per serving** (TOTAL : Serves)

❄ **Seasonal**
- ☐ spring
- ☐ summer
- ☐ fall
- ☐ winter
- ☐ year round

🍴 **Utensils**

○ baking dish	○ grater	○ revolving cake stand
○ baking paper	○ kitchen scissors	○ rolling pin
○ baking tin	○ kitchen torch	○ rubber spatula
○ baking tray	○ knife	○ sieve
○ blender	○ ladle	○ skimmer
○ bowl	○ measuring cups set	○ soucepan
○ cake scraper	○ measuring spoons set	○ spoon
○ chopping board	○ mixer	○ squeezer
○ cling film	○ mold	○ strainer
○ cookie cutter	○ offset spatula	○ teaspoon
○ cooking pan	○ pasta roller	○ weight scale
○ cooling rack	○ pasta wheel	○ whisk
○ cup	○ pastry brush	○
○ digital thermometer	○ piping bag	○
○ dough mixer	○ piping nozzle	○
○ electric whisk	○ pot	○
○ fork	○ potato peeler	○

🍴 **Special diet**
- ☐ egg-free
- ☐ fat-free
- ☐ gluten-free
- ☐ lactose-free
- ☐ sugar-free
- ☐ vegan
- ☐ vegetarian
- ☐ ____

Instructions

Procedure | Time
- [ ] cooking
- [ ] cooling
- [ ] decorating
- [ ] freezing
- [ ] prepping
- [ ] proofing
- [ ] rest
- [ ]

TOT time

Cooking | temp. | time
- [ ] bain-marie
- [ ] cooktop
- [ ] fan oven
- [ ] fryer
- [ ] grill
- [ ] microwave
- [ ] static oven
- [ ]

Preservation | temp. | time
- [ ] freezer
- [ ] fridge
- [ ] room temp.
- [ ]

container
- [ ] airtight container
- [ ] cling film
- [ ] food-grade bag
- [ ]

Notes

Picture

Memo

Recipes used
- Vol.
- Vol.
- Vol.
- Vol.

Recipe's variants
- Vol.
- Vol.

Recipe

Difficulty ☐☐☐☐☐   Rating ☆☆☆☆☆   📅 Date ....

author ....

🚩 Nationality ....   🎂 Dimensions ....   ⚖ Weight ....   🍪 Pieces ....   👥 Serves ....

🧁 Type of dessert
- ☐ basic recipe
- ☐ cake
- ☐ chocolate
- ☐ cookie
- ☐ fried
- ☐ leavened
- ☐ pastry
- ☐ pie
- ☐ tart
- ☐ ....

🎉 Ideal for
- ☐ breakfast
- ☐ dessert
- ☐ snacks
- ☐ occasion
- ☐ ....

❄ Seasonal
- ☐ spring
- ☐ summer
- ☐ fall
- ☐ winter
- ☐ year round

🍴 Special diet
- ☐ egg-free
- ☐ fat-free
- ☐ gluten-free
- ☐ lactose-free
- ☐ sugar-free
- ☐ vegan
- ☐ vegetarian
- ☐ ....

check	🍶 Ingredients	⚖ Quantity (Q)	Percentage (%=Q:T×100)	💰 Cost
○				
○				
○				
○				
○				
○				
○				
○				
○				
○				
○				
○				
○				
○				
○				
○				

🎂 **TOTAL** (Σ column values)   (T).............. 100%

👥 **Per serving** (TOTAL : Serves) ....

🍴 Utensils

- ○ baking dish
- ○ baking paper
- ○ baking tin
- ○ baking tray
- ○ blender
- ○ bowl
- ○ cake scraper
- ○ chopping board
- ○ cling film
- ○ cookie cutter
- ○ cooking pan
- ○ cooling rack
- ○ cup
- ○ digital thermometer
- ○ dough mixer
- ○ electric whisk
- ○ fork
- ○ grater
- ○ kitchen scissors
- ○ kitchen torch
- ○ knife
- ○ ladle
- ○ measuring cups set
- ○ measuring spoons set
- ○ mixer
- ○ mold
- ○ offset spatula
- ○ pasta roller
- ○ pasta wheel
- ○ pastry brush
- ○ piping bag
- ○ piping nozzle
- ○ pot
- ○ potato peeler
- ○ revolving cake stand
- ○ rolling pin
- ○ rubber spatula
- ○ sieve
- ○ skimmer
- ○ soucepan
- ○ spoon
- ○ squeezer
- ○ strainer
- ○ teaspoon
- ○ weight scale
- ○ whisk
- ○
- ○
- ○
- ○

Instructions

Procedure | Time
- [ ] cooking
- [ ] cooling
- [ ] decorating
- [ ] freezing
- [ ] prepping
- [ ] proofing
- [ ] rest
- [ ]

TOT time

Cooking | temp. | time
- [ ] bain-marie
- [ ] cooktop
- [ ] fan oven
- [ ] fryer
- [ ] grill
- [ ] microwave
- [ ] static oven
- [ ]

Preservation | temp. | time
- [ ] freezer
- [ ] fridge
- [ ] room temp.
- [ ]

container
- [ ] airtight container
- [ ] cling film
- [ ] food-grade bag
- [ ]

Notes

Recipes used
- Vol.
- Vol.
- Vol.
- Vol.

Recipe's variants
- Vol.
- Vol.

Picture

Memo

Recipe

Difficulty ☗☗☗☗☗ **Rating** ☆☆☆☆☆ 📅 **Date**

author

🚩 **Nationality** 🎂 Dimensions ⚖️ Weight 🍪 Pieces 👥 **Serves**

🧁 **Type** of dessert
- ☐ basic recipe
- ☐ cake
- ☐ chocolate
- ☐ cookie
- ☐ fried
- ☐ leavened
- ☐ pastry
- ☐ pie
- ☐ tart
- ☐

🎉 **Ideal for**
- ☐ breakfast
- ☐ dessert
- ☐ snacks
- ☐ occasion

☐

❄️ **Seasonal**
- ☐ spring
- ☐ summer
- ☐ fall
- ☐ winter
- ☐ year round

🍴 **Special diet**
- ☐ egg-free
- ☐ fat-free
- ☐ gluten-free
- ☐ lactose-free
- ☐ sugar-free
- ☐ vegan
- ☐ vegetarian
- ☐

check ✓ 🍯 **Ingredients**   ⚖️ Quantity (Q) Percentage (%=Q:Tx100) 💰 Cost

🎂 **TOTAL** (Σ column values)   (T)............ 100%
👥 **Per serving** (TOTAL : Serves)

🍴 **Utensils**
- ○ baking dish
- ○ baking paper
- ○ baking tin
- ○ baking tray
- ○ blender
- ○ bowl
- ○ cake scraper
- ○ chopping board
- ○ cling film
- ○ cookie cutter
- ○ cooking pan
- ○ cooling rack
- ○ cup
- ○ digital thermometer
- ○ dough mixer
- ○ electric whisk
- ○ fork
- ○ grater
- ○ kitchen scissors
- ○ kitchen torch
- ○ knife
- ○ ladle
- ○ measuring cups set
- ○ measuring spoons set
- ○ mixer
- ○ mold
- ○ offset spatula
- ○ pasta roller
- ○ pasta wheel
- ○ pastry brush
- ○ piping bag
- ○ piping nozzle
- ○ pot
- ○ potato peeler
- ○ revolving cake stand
- ○ rolling pin
- ○ rubber spatula
- ○ sieve
- ○ skimmer
- ○ soucepan
- ○ spoon
- ○ squeezer
- ○ strainer
- ○ teaspoon
- ○ weight scale
- ○ whisk
- ○
- ○

Instructions

Procedure | Time
- [ ] cooking
- [ ] cooling
- [ ] decorating
- [ ] freezing
- [ ] prepping
- [ ] proofing
- [ ] rest
- [ ]

TOT time

Cooking | temp. | time
- [ ] bain-marie
- [ ] cooktop
- [ ] fan oven
- [ ] fryer
- [ ] grill
- [ ] microwave
- [ ] static oven
- [ ]

Preservation | temp. | time
- [ ] freezer
- [ ] fridge
- [ ] room temp.
- [ ]

container
- [ ] airtight container
- [ ] cling film
- [ ] food-grade bag
- [ ]

Notes

Recipes used
- Vol.
- Vol.
- Vol.
- Vol.

Recipe's variants
- Vol.
- Vol.

Picture

Memo

Recipe

Difficulty ♡♡♡♡♡ **Rating** ☆☆☆☆☆ 📅 **Date** ....

....

author ....

🚩 **Nationality** .... 📦 **Dimensions** .... ⚖️ **Weight** .... 🍪 **Pieces** .... 👥 **Serves** ....

🧁 **Type** of dessert
- ☐ basic recipe
- ☐ cake
- ☐ chocolate
- ☐ cookie
- ☐ fried
- ☐ leavened
- ☐ pastry
- ☐ pie
- ☐ tart
- ☐ ....

🎉 **Ideal for**
- ☐ breakfast
- ☐ dessert
- ☐ snacks
- ☐ occasion
- ☐ ....

❄️ **Seasonal**
- ☐ spring
- ☐ summer
- ☐ fall
- ☐ winter
- ☐ year round

🍴 **Special diet**
- ☐ egg-free
- ☐ fat-free
- ☐ gluten-free
- ☐ lactose-free
- ☐ sugar-free
- ☐ vegan
- ☐ vegetarian
- ☐ ....

check	🍯 **Ingredients**	⚖️ Quantity (Q)	Percentage (%=Q:T×100)	💰 Cost
○				
○				
○				
○				
○				
○				
○				
○				
○				
○				
○				
○				
○				
○				

🎂 **TOTAL** (Σ column values) .... (T) .... 100% ....

👥 **Per serving** (TOTAL : Serves) ....

🍴 **Utensils**
- ○ baking dish
- ○ baking paper
- ○ baking tin
- ○ baking tray
- ○ blender
- ○ bowl
- ○ cake scraper
- ○ chopping board
- ○ cling film
- ○ cookie cutter
- ○ cooking pan
- ○ cooling rack
- ○ cup
- ○ digital thermometer
- ○ dough mixer
- ○ electric whisk
- ○ fork
- ○ grater
- ○ kitchen scissors
- ○ kitchen torch
- ○ knife
- ○ ladle
- ○ measuring cups set
- ○ measuring spoons set
- ○ mixer
- ○ mold
- ○ offset spatula
- ○ pasta roller
- ○ pasta wheel
- ○ pastry brush
- ○ piping bag
- ○ piping nozzle
- ○ pot
- ○ potato peeler
- ○ revolving cake stand
- ○ rolling pin
- ○ rubber spatula
- ○ sieve
- ○ skimmer
- ○ soucepan
- ○ spoon
- ○ squeezer
- ○ strainer
- ○ teaspoon
- ○ weight scale
- ○ whisk
- ○ ....
- ○ ....
- ○ ....

Instructions

Procedure / Time
- [ ] cooking
- [ ] cooling
- [ ] decorating
- [ ] freezing
- [ ] prepping
- [ ] proofing
- [ ] rest
- [ ]

TOT time

Cooking — temp. / time
- [ ] bain-marie
- [ ] cooktop
- [ ] fan oven
- [ ] fryer
- [ ] grill
- [ ] microwave
- [ ] static oven
- [ ]

Preservation — temp. / time
- [ ] freezer
- [ ] fridge
- [ ] room temp.
- [ ]

container
- [ ] airtight container
- [ ] cling film
- [ ] food-grade bag
- [ ]

Notes

Recipes used
- Vol.
- Vol.
- Vol.
- Vol.

Recipe's variants
- Vol.
- Vol.

Picture

Memo

Recipe

Difficulty ♕♕♕♕♕ Rating ☆☆☆☆☆   📅 Date ....

.... author ....

🚩 Nationality ....   🎂 Dimensions ....   ⚖️ Weight ....   🍪 Pieces ....   👥 Serves ....

🧁 Type of dessert
- ☐ basic recipe
- ☐ cake
- ☐ chocolate
- ☐ cookie
- ☐ fried
- ☐ leavened
- ☐ pastry
- ☐ pie
- ☐ tart
- ☐ ....

🎉 Ideal for
- ☐ breakfast
- ☐ dessert
- ☐ snacks
- ☐ occasion
- ☐ ....

❄️ Seasonal
- ☐ spring
- ☐ summer
- ☐ fall
- ☐ winter
- ☐ year round

🍴 Special diet
- ☐ egg-free
- ☐ fat-free
- ☐ gluten-free
- ☐ lactose-free
- ☐ sugar-free
- ☐ vegan
- ☐ vegetarian
- ☐ ....

check ✓ | 🥫 Ingredients | ⚖️ Quantity (Q) | Percentage (%=Q:T×100) | 💰 Cost

TOTAL (Σ column values) .... (T) 100%

👥 **Per serving** (TOTAL : Serves) ....

🍴 Utensils
- ○ baking dish
- ○ baking paper
- ○ baking tin
- ○ baking tray
- ○ blender
- ○ bowl
- ○ cake scraper
- ○ chopping board
- ○ cling film
- ○ cookie cutter
- ○ cooking pan
- ○ cooling rack
- ○ cup
- ○ digital thermometer
- ○ dough mixer
- ○ electric whisk
- ○ fork
- ○ grater
- ○ kitchen scissors
- ○ kitchen torch
- ○ knife
- ○ ladle
- ○ measuring cups set
- ○ measuring spoons set
- ○ mixer
- ○ mold
- ○ offset spatula
- ○ pasta roller
- ○ pasta wheel
- ○ pastry brush
- ○ piping bag
- ○ piping nozzle
- ○ pot
- ○ potato peeler
- ○ revolving cake stand
- ○ rolling pin
- ○ rubber spatula
- ○ sieve
- ○ skimmer
- ○ soucepan
- ○ spoon
- ○ squeezer
- ○ strainer
- ○ teaspoon
- ○ weight scale
- ○ whisk
- ○ ....
- ○ ....

Instructions

Procedure | Time
- [ ] cooking
- [ ] cooling
- [ ] decorating
- [ ] freezing
- [ ] prepping
- [ ] proofing
- [ ] rest
- [ ]

TOT time

Cooking | temp. | time
- [ ] bain-marie
- [ ] cooktop
- [ ] fan oven
- [ ] fryer
- [ ] grill
- [ ] microwave
- [ ] static oven
- [ ]

Preservation | temp. | time
- [ ] freezer
- [ ] fridge
- [ ] room temp.
- [ ]

container
- [ ] airtight container
- [ ] cling film
- [ ] food-grade bag
- [ ]

Notes

Recipes used
- Vol.
- Vol.
- Vol.
- Vol.

Recipe's variants
- Vol.
- Vol.

Picture

Memo

Recipe

Difficulty ☁☁☁☁☁   **Rating** ☆☆☆☆☆   📅 **Date** ....

....

author ....

🚩 **Nationality** ....   🎂 **Dimensions** ....   ⚖️ **Weight** ....   🍪 **Pieces** ....   👥 **Serves** ....

🧁 **Type** of dessert
- ☐ basic recipe
- ☐ cake
- ☐ chocolate
- ☐ cookie
- ☐ fried
- ☐ leavened
- ☐ pastry
- ☐ pie
- ☐ tart
- ☐ ....

🎉 **Ideal for**
- ☐ breakfast
- ☐ dessert
- ☐ snacks
- ☐ occasion
- ☐ ....

❄️ **Seasonal**
- ☐ spring
- ☐ summer
- ☐ fall
- ☐ winter
- ☐ year round

🍴 **Special diet**
- ☐ egg-free
- ☐ fat-free
- ☐ gluten-free
- ☐ lactose-free
- ☐ sugar-free
- ☐ vegan
- ☐ vegetarian
- ☐ ....

check	🍯 **Ingredients**	⚖️ Quantity (Q)	Percentage (%=Q:T×100)	🪙 Cost
○				
○				
○				
○				
○				
○				
○				
○				
○				
○				
○				
○				
○				

🎂 **TOTAL** (Σ column values) .... (T) 100%

👥 **Per serving** (TOTAL : Serves) ....

🥄 **Utensils**

- ○ baking dish
- ○ baking paper
- ○ baking tin
- ○ baking tray
- ○ blender
- ○ bowl
- ○ cake scraper
- ○ chopping board
- ○ cling film
- ○ cookie cutter
- ○ cooking pan
- ○ cooling rack
- ○ cup
- ○ digital thermometer
- ○ dough mixer
- ○ electric whisk
- ○ fork
- ○ grater
- ○ kitchen scissors
- ○ kitchen torch
- ○ knife
- ○ ladle
- ○ measuring cups set
- ○ measuring spoons set
- ○ mixer
- ○ mold
- ○ offset spatula
- ○ pasta roller
- ○ pasta wheel
- ○ pastry brush
- ○ piping bag
- ○ piping nozzle
- ○ pot
- ○ potato peeler
- ○ revolving cake stand
- ○ rolling pin
- ○ rubber spatula
- ○ sieve
- ○ skimmer
- ○ soucepan
- ○ spoon
- ○ squeezer
- ○ strainer
- ○ teaspoon
- ○ weight scale
- ○ whisk
- ○ ....
- ○ ....
- ○ ....

Instructions

Procedure | Time
- [ ] cooking
- [ ] cooling
- [ ] decorating
- [ ] freezing
- [ ] prepping
- [ ] proofing
- [ ] rest
- [ ]

TOT time

Cooking | temp. | time
- [ ] bain-marie
- [ ] cooktop
- [ ] fan oven
- [ ] fryer
- [ ] grill
- [ ] microwave
- [ ] static oven
- [ ]

Preservation | temp. | time
- [ ] freezer
- [ ] fridge
- [ ] room temp.
- [ ]

container
- [ ] airtight container
- [ ] cling film
- [ ] food-grade bag
- [ ]

Notes

Recipes used
- Vol.
- Vol.
- Vol.
- Vol.

Recipe's variants
- Vol.
- Vol.

Picture

Memo

Recipe

Difficulty ♙♙♙♙♙   Rating ☆☆☆☆☆   📅 Date _____

_____   author _____

🚩 Nationality _____   🎂 Dimensions _____   ⚖️ Weight _____   🍪 Pieces _____   👥 Serves _____

🧁 **Type** of dessert
- ☐ basic recipe
- ☐ cake
- ☐ chocolate
- ☐ cookie
- ☐ fried
- ☐ leavened
- ☐ pastry
- ☐ pie
- ☐ tart
- ☐ _____

🎉 **Ideal for**
- ☐ breakfast
- ☐ dessert
- ☐ snacks
- ☐ occasion

☐ _____

❄️ **Seasonal**
- ☐ spring
- ☐ summer
- ☐ fall
- ☐ winter
- ☐ year round

🍴 **Special diet**
- ☐ egg-free
- ☐ fat-free
- ☐ gluten-free
- ☐ lactose-free
- ☐ sugar-free
- ☐ vegan
- ☐ vegetarian

☐ _____

check ✓   🍯 **Ingredients**   ⚖️ Quantity (Q)   Percentage (%=Q:T×100)   💰 Cost

(ingredient rows with ○ checkboxes)

🎂 **TOTAL** (Σ column values) _____ (T) _____ 100%
👥 **Per serving** (TOTAL : Serves) _____

🍴 **Utensils**
- ○ baking dish
- ○ baking paper
- ○ baking tin
- ○ baking tray
- ○ blender
- ○ bowl
- ○ cake scraper
- ○ chopping board
- ○ cling film
- ○ cookie cutter
- ○ cooking pan
- ○ cooling rack
- ○ cup
- ○ digital thermometer
- ○ dough mixer
- ○ electric whisk
- ○ fork
- ○ grater
- ○ kitchen scissors
- ○ kitchen torch
- ○ knife
- ○ ladle
- ○ measuring cups set
- ○ measuring spoons set
- ○ mixer
- ○ mold
- ○ offset spatula
- ○ pasta roller
- ○ pasta wheel
- ○ pastry brush
- ○ piping bag
- ○ piping nozzle
- ○ pot
- ○ potato peeler
- ○ revolving cake stand
- ○ rolling pin
- ○ rubber spatula
- ○ sieve
- ○ skimmer
- ○ soucepan
- ○ spoon
- ○ squeezer
- ○ strainer
- ○ teaspoon
- ○ weight scale
- ○ whisk
- ○ _____
- ○ _____

Instructions

Procedure | Time
- [ ] cooking
- [ ] cooling
- [ ] decorating
- [ ] freezing
- [ ] prepping
- [ ] proofing
- [ ] rest
- [ ]

TOT time

Cooking | temp. | time
- [ ] bain-marie
- [ ] cooktop
- [ ] fan oven
- [ ] fryer
- [ ] grill
- [ ] microwave
- [ ] static oven
- [ ]

Preservation | temp. | time
- [ ] freezer
- [ ] fridge
- [ ] room temp.
- [ ]

container
- [ ] airtight container
- [ ] cling film
- [ ] food-grade bag
- [ ]

Notes

Recipes used
- Vol.
- Vol.
- Vol.
- Vol.

Recipe's variants
- Vol.
- Vol.

Picture

Memo

Recipe

Difficulty ♕♕♕♕♕ Rating ☆☆☆☆☆ 📅 Date _____

_____ author _____

🚩 Nationality _____ 🎂 Dimensions _____ ⚖ Weight _____ 🍪 Pieces _____ 👥 Serves _____

🧁 Type of dessert
- ☐ basic recipe
- ☐ cake
- ☐ chocolate
- ☐ cookie
- ☐ fried
- ☐ leavened
- ☐ pastry
- ☐ pie
- ☐ tart
- ☐ _____

🎉 Ideal for
- ☐ breakfast
- ☐ dessert
- ☐ snacks
- ☐ occasion
- ☐ _____

❄ Seasonal
- ☐ spring
- ☐ summer
- ☐ fall
- ☐ winter
- ☐ year round

🍴 Special diet
- ☐ egg-free
- ☐ fat-free
- ☐ gluten-free
- ☐ lactose-free
- ☐ sugar-free
- ☐ vegan
- ☐ vegetarian
- ☐ _____

🧴 Ingredients

check	Ingredients	Quantity (Q)	Percentage (%=Q:T×100)	Cost
○				
○				
○				
○				
○				
○				
○				
○				
○				
○				
○				
○				
○				
○				

🎂 **TOTAL** (Σ column values) _____ (T) _____ 100%

👥 **Per serving** (TOTAL : Serves) _____

🍴 Utensils
- ○ baking dish
- ○ baking paper
- ○ baking tin
- ○ baking tray
- ○ blender
- ○ bowl
- ○ cake scraper
- ○ chopping board
- ○ cling film
- ○ cookie cutter
- ○ cooking pan
- ○ cooling rack
- ○ cup
- ○ digital thermometer
- ○ dough mixer
- ○ electric whisk
- ○ fork
- ○ grater
- ○ kitchen scissors
- ○ kitchen torch
- ○ knife
- ○ ladle
- ○ measuring cups set
- ○ measuring spoons set
- ○ mixer
- ○ mold
- ○ offset spatula
- ○ pasta roller
- ○ pasta wheel
- ○ pastry brush
- ○ piping bag
- ○ piping nozzle
- ○ pot
- ○ potato peeler
- ○ revolving cake stand
- ○ rolling pin
- ○ rubber spatula
- ○ sieve
- ○ skimmer
- ○ soucepan
- ○ spoon
- ○ squeezer
- ○ strainer
- ○ teaspoon
- ○ weight scale
- ○ whisk
- ○ _____
- ○ _____
- ○ _____

Instructions

Procedure | Time
- [ ] cooking
- [ ] cooling
- [ ] decorating
- [ ] freezing
- [ ] prepping
- [ ] proofing
- [ ] rest
- [ ]

TOT time

Cooking | temp. | time
- [ ] bain-marie
- [ ] cooktop
- [ ] fan oven
- [ ] fryer
- [ ] grill
- [ ] microwave
- [ ] static oven
- [ ]

Preservation | temp. | time
- [ ] freezer
- [ ] fridge
- [ ] room temp.
- [ ]

container
- [ ] airtight container
- [ ] cling film
- [ ] food-grade bag
- [ ]

Notes

Picture

Memo

Recipes used
- Vol.
- Vol.
- Vol.
- Vol.

Recipe's variants
- Vol.
- Vol.

Recipe

Difficulty ☷☷☷☷☷ **Rating** ☆☆☆☆☆   📅 **Date** ....

.... author ....

🚩 **Nationality** .... 🎂 Dimensions .... ⚖️ Weight .... 🍪 Pieces .... 👥 **Serves** ....

🧁 **Type** of dessert
- ☐ basic recipe
- ☐ cake
- ☐ chocolate
- ☐ cookie
- ☐ fried
- ☐ leavened
- ☐ pastry
- ☐ pie
- ☐ tart
- ☐ ....

🎉 **Ideal for**
- ☐ breakfast
- ☐ dessert
- ☐ snacks
- ☐ occasion

☐ ....

❄️ **Seasonal**
- ☐ spring
- ☐ summer
- ☐ fall
- ☐ winter
- ☐ year round

🍴 **Special diet**
- ☐ egg-free
- ☐ fat-free
- ☐ gluten-free
- ☐ lactose-free
- ☐ sugar-free
- ☐ vegan
- ☐ vegetarian
- ☐ ....

check	🫙 **Ingredients**	⚖️ Quantity (Q)	Percentage (%=Q:T×100)	💰 Cost
○				
○				
○				
○				
○				
○				
○				
○				
○				
○				
○				
○				
○				
○				
○				

🎂 **TOTAL** (Σ column values) .... (T).......... 100% ....

👥 **Per serving** (TOTAL : Serves) ....

🍴 **Utensils**
- ○ baking dish
- ○ baking paper
- ○ baking tin
- ○ baking tray
- ○ blender
- ○ bowl
- ○ cake scraper
- ○ chopping board
- ○ cling film
- ○ cookie cutter
- ○ cooking pan
- ○ cooling rack
- ○ cup
- ○ digital thermometer
- ○ dough mixer
- ○ electric whisk
- ○ fork
- ○ grater
- ○ kitchen scissors
- ○ kitchen torch
- ○ knife
- ○ ladle
- ○ measuring cups set
- ○ measuring spoons set
- ○ mixer
- ○ mold
- ○ offset spatula
- ○ pasta roller
- ○ pasta wheel
- ○ pastry brush
- ○ piping bag
- ○ piping nozzle
- ○ pot
- ○ potato peeler
- ○ revolving cake stand
- ○ rolling pin
- ○ rubber spatula
- ○ sieve
- ○ skimmer
- ○ soucepan
- ○ spoon
- ○ squeezer
- ○ strainer
- ○ teaspoon
- ○ weight scale
- ○ whisk
- ○ ....
- ○ ....
- ○ ....

Instructions

Procedure | Time
- [ ] cooking
- [ ] cooling
- [ ] decorating
- [ ] freezing
- [ ] prepping
- [ ] proofing
- [ ] rest
- [ ]

TOT time

Cooking | temp. | time
- [ ] bain-marie
- [ ] cooktop
- [ ] fan oven
- [ ] fryer
- [ ] grill
- [ ] microwave
- [ ] static oven
- [ ]

Preservation | temp. | time
- [ ] freezer
- [ ] fridge
- [ ] room temp.
- [ ]

container
- [ ] airtight container
- [ ] cling film
- [ ] food-grade bag
- [ ]

Notes

Recipes used
- Vol.
- Vol.
- Vol.
- Vol.

Recipe's variants
- Vol.
- Vol.

Picture

Memo

Recipe

Difficulty 👨‍🍳👨‍🍳👨‍🍳👨‍🍳👨‍🍳 Rating ☆☆☆☆☆ 📅 Date ....

.... *author* ....

🚩 **Nationality** .... 📦 Dimensions .... ⚖ Weight .... 🍪 Pieces .... 👥 **Serves** ....

🧁 Type of dessert
- [ ] basic recipe
- [ ] cake
- [ ] chocolate
- [ ] cookie
- [ ] fried
- [ ] leavened
- [ ] pastry
- [ ] pie
- [ ] tart
- [ ] ....

🎉 Ideal for
- [ ] breakfast
- [ ] dessert
- [ ] snacks
- [ ] occasion

- [ ] ....

❄ Seasonal
- [ ] spring
- [ ] summer
- [ ] fall
- [ ] winter
- [ ] year round

🍴 Special diet
- [ ] egg-free
- [ ] fat-free
- [ ] gluten-free
- [ ] lactose-free
- [ ] sugar-free
- [ ] vegan
- [ ] vegetarian
- [ ] ....

Ingredients

check	Ingredients	Quantity (Q)	Percentage (%=Q:T×100)	Cost
○				
○				
○				
○				
○				
○				
○				
○				
○				
○				
○				
○				
○				
○				

🎂 **TOTAL** (Σ column values) .... (T) 100%

👥 **Per serving** (TOTAL : Serves) ....

🍴 Utensils

- ○ baking dish
- ○ baking paper
- ○ baking tin
- ○ baking tray
- ○ blender
- ○ bowl
- ○ cake scraper
- ○ chopping board
- ○ cling film
- ○ cookie cutter
- ○ cooking pan
- ○ cooling rack
- ○ cup
- ○ digital thermometer
- ○ dough mixer
- ○ electric whisk
- ○ fork
- ○ grater
- ○ kitchen scissors
- ○ kitchen torch
- ○ knife
- ○ ladle
- ○ measuring cups set
- ○ measuring spoons set
- ○ mixer
- ○ mold
- ○ offset spatula
- ○ pasta roller
- ○ pasta wheel
- ○ pastry brush
- ○ piping bag
- ○ piping nozzle
- ○ pot
- ○ potato peeler
- ○ revolving cake stand
- ○ rolling pin
- ○ rubber spatula
- ○ sieve
- ○ skimmer
- ○ soucepan
- ○ spoon
- ○ squeezer
- ○ strainer
- ○ teaspoon
- ○ weight scale
- ○ whisk
- ○ ....
- ○ ....
- ○ ....

Instructions

Procedure | Time
- [ ] cooking
- [ ] cooling
- [ ] decorating
- [ ] freezing
- [ ] prepping
- [ ] proofing
- [ ] rest
- [ ]

TOT time

Cooking — temp. | time
- [ ] bain-marie
- [ ] cooktop
- [ ] fan oven
- [ ] fryer
- [ ] grill
- [ ] microwave
- [ ] static oven
- [ ]

Preservation — temp. | time
- [ ] freezer
- [ ] fridge
- [ ] room temp.
- [ ]

container
- [ ] airtight container
- [ ] cling film
- [ ] food-grade bag
- [ ]

Notes

Recipes used
- Vol.
- Vol.
- Vol.
- Vol.

Recipe's variants
- Vol.
- Vol.

Picture

Memo

Recipe

Difficulty ♟♟♟♟♟ Rating ☆☆☆☆☆   📅 Date ....

.... author ....

🚩 Nationality .... 🎂 Dimensions .... ⚖ Weight .... 🍪 Pieces .... 👥 Serves ....

🧁 Type of dessert
- ☐ basic recipe
- ☐ cake
- ☐ chocolate
- ☐ cookie
- ☐ fried
- ☐ leavened
- ☐ pastry
- ☐ pie
- ☐ tart
- ☐ ....

🎉 Ideal for
- ☐ breakfast
- ☐ dessert
- ☐ snacks
- ☐ occasion

☐ ....

❄ Seasonal
- ☐ spring
- ☐ summer
- ☐ fall
- ☐ winter
- ☐ year round

🍴 Special diet
- ☐ egg-free
- ☐ fat-free
- ☐ gluten-free
- ☐ lactose-free
- ☐ sugar-free
- ☐ vegan
- ☐ vegetarian
- ☐ ....

check 🍯 Ingredients   ⚖ Quantity (Q)   Percentage (%=Q:T×100)   🪙 Cost

check	Ingredients	Quantity (Q)	Percentage (%=Q:T×100)	Cost
○				
○				
○				
○				
○				
○				
○				
○				
○				
○				
○				
○				
○				
○				

🎂 **TOTAL** (Σ column values) .... (T) 100%

👥 **Per serving** (TOTAL : Serves) ....

🍴 Utensils

- ○ baking dish
- ○ baking paper
- ○ baking tin
- ○ baking tray
- ○ blender
- ○ bowl
- ○ cake scraper
- ○ chopping board
- ○ cling film
- ○ cookie cutter
- ○ cooking pan
- ○ cooling rack
- ○ cup
- ○ digital thermometer
- ○ dough mixer
- ○ electric whisk
- ○ fork
- ○ grater
- ○ kitchen scissors
- ○ kitchen torch
- ○ knife
- ○ ladle
- ○ measuring cups set
- ○ measuring spoons set
- ○ mixer
- ○ mold
- ○ offset spatula
- ○ pasta roller
- ○ pasta wheel
- ○ pastry brush
- ○ piping bag
- ○ piping nozzle
- ○ pot
- ○ potato peeler
- ○ revolving cake stand
- ○ rolling pin
- ○ rubber spatula
- ○ sieve
- ○ skimmer
- ○ soucepan
- ○ spoon
- ○ squeezer
- ○ strainer
- ○ teaspoon
- ○ weight scale
- ○ whisk
- ○ ....
- ○ ....
- ○ ....

Instructions

Procedure | Time
- [ ] cooking
- [ ] cooling
- [ ] decorating
- [ ] freezing
- [ ] prepping
- [ ] proofing
- [ ] rest
- [ ]

TOT time

Cooking | temp. | time
- [ ] bain-marie
- [ ] cooktop
- [ ] fan oven
- [ ] fryer
- [ ] grill
- [ ] microwave
- [ ] static oven
- [ ]

Preservation | temp. | time
- [ ] freezer
- [ ] fridge
- [ ] room temp.
- [ ]

container
- [ ] airtight container
- [ ] cling film
- [ ] food-grade bag
- [ ]

Notes

Recipes used
- Vol.
- Vol.
- Vol.
- Vol.

Recipe's variants
- Vol.
- Vol.

Picture

Memo

Recipe

Difficulty ☷☷☷☷☷ **Rating** ☆☆☆☆☆ 📅 **Date** ....

.... author ....

🚩 **Nationality** .... 🎂 Dimensions .... ⚖ Weight .... 🍪 Pieces .... 👥 **Serves** ....

🧁 **Type** of dessert
- [ ] basic recipe
- [ ] cake
- [ ] chocolate
- [ ] cookie
- [ ] fried
- [ ] leavened
- [ ] pastry
- [ ] pie
- [ ] tart
- [ ] ....

🎉 **Ideal for**
- [ ] breakfast
- [ ] dessert
- [ ] snacks
- [ ] occasion

- [ ] ....

❄ **Seasonal**
- [ ] spring
- [ ] summer
- [ ] fall
- [ ] winter
- [ ] year round

🍴 **Special diet**
- [ ] egg-free
- [ ] fat-free
- [ ] gluten-free
- [ ] lactose-free
- [ ] sugar-free
- [ ] vegan
- [ ] vegetarian
- [ ] ....

check	🍶 **Ingredients**	⚖ Quantity (Q)	Percentage (%=Q:Tx100)	💰 Cost
○				
○				
○				
○				
○				
○				
○				
○				
○				
○				
○				
○				
○				
○				

🎂 **TOTAL** (Σ column values) .... (T) .... 100% ....

👥 **Per serving** (TOTAL : Serves) ....

🍴 **Utensils**

- ○ baking dish
- ○ baking paper
- ○ baking tin
- ○ baking tray
- ○ blender
- ○ bowl
- ○ cake scraper
- ○ chopping board
- ○ cling film
- ○ cookie cutter
- ○ cooking pan
- ○ cooling rack
- ○ cup
- ○ digital thermometer
- ○ dough mixer
- ○ electric whisk
- ○ fork
- ○ grater
- ○ kitchen scissors
- ○ kitchen torch
- ○ knife
- ○ ladle
- ○ measuring cups set
- ○ measuring spoons set
- ○ mixer
- ○ mold
- ○ offset spatula
- ○ pasta roller
- ○ pasta wheel
- ○ pastry brush
- ○ piping bag
- ○ piping nozzle
- ○ pot
- ○ potato peeler
- ○ revolving cake stand
- ○ rolling pin
- ○ rubber spatula
- ○ sieve
- ○ skimmer
- ○ soucepan
- ○ spoon
- ○ squeezer
- ○ strainer
- ○ teaspoon
- ○ weight scale
- ○ whisk
- ○ ....
- ○ ....
- ○ ....

Instructions

Procedure | Time
- [ ] cooking
- [ ] cooling
- [ ] decorating
- [ ] freezing
- [ ] prepping
- [ ] proofing
- [ ] rest
- [ ]

TOT time

Cooking | temp. | time
- [ ] bain-marie
- [ ] cooktop
- [ ] fan oven
- [ ] fryer
- [ ] grill
- [ ] microwave
- [ ] static oven
- [ ]

Preservation | temp. | time
- [ ] freezer
- [ ] fridge
- [ ] room temp.
- [ ]

container
- [ ] airtight container
- [ ] cling film
- [ ] food-grade bag
- [ ]

Recipes used
- Vol.
- Vol.
- Vol.
- Vol.

Recipe's variants
- Vol.
- Vol.

Notes

Picture

Memo

Recipe

Difficulty 🎩🎩🎩🎩🎩   Rating ☆☆☆☆☆   📅 Date _____

_____   author _____

🚩 **Nationality** _____   🍰 Dimensions _____   ⚖️ Weight _____   🍪 Pieces _____   👥 **Serves** _____

🧁 **Type** of dessert
- [ ] basic recipe
- [ ] cake
- [ ] chocolate
- [ ] cookie
- [ ] fried
- [ ] leavened
- [ ] pastry
- [ ] pie
- [ ] tart
- [ ] _____

🎉 **Ideal for**
- [ ] breakfast
- [ ] dessert
- [ ] snacks
- [ ] occasion
- [ ] _____

❄️ **Seasonal**
- [ ] spring
- [ ] summer
- [ ] fall
- [ ] winter
- [ ] year round

🍴 **Special diet**
- [ ] egg-free
- [ ] fat-free
- [ ] gluten-free
- [ ] lactose-free
- [ ] sugar-free
- [ ] vegan
- [ ] vegetarian
- [ ] _____

check ✓

🧂 **Ingredients** | Quantity (Q) | Percentage (%=Q:T×100) | 💰 Cost

🎂 **TOTAL** (Σ column values)   (T) _____   100%

👥 **Per serving** (TOTAL : Serves)

🍴 **Utensils**
- ○ baking dish
- ○ baking paper
- ○ baking tin
- ○ baking tray
- ○ blender
- ○ bowl
- ○ cake scraper
- ○ chopping board
- ○ cling film
- ○ cookie cutter
- ○ cooking pan
- ○ cooling rack
- ○ cup
- ○ digital thermometer
- ○ dough mixer
- ○ electric whisk
- ○ fork
- ○ grater
- ○ kitchen scissors
- ○ kitchen torch
- ○ knife
- ○ ladle
- ○ measuring cups set
- ○ measuring spoons set
- ○ mixer
- ○ mold
- ○ offset spatula
- ○ pasta roller
- ○ pasta wheel
- ○ pastry brush
- ○ piping bag
- ○ piping nozzle
- ○ pot
- ○ potato peeler
- ○ revolving cake stand
- ○ rolling pin
- ○ rubber spatula
- ○ sieve
- ○ skimmer
- ○ soucepan
- ○ spoon
- ○ squeezer
- ○ strainer
- ○ teaspoon
- ○ weight scale
- ○ whisk

Instructions

Procedure | Time
- [ ] cooking
- [ ] cooling
- [ ] decorating
- [ ] freezing
- [ ] prepping
- [ ] proofing
- [ ] rest
- [ ]

TOT time

Cooking | temp. | time
- [ ] bain-marie
- [ ] cooktop
- [ ] fan oven
- [ ] fryer
- [ ] grill
- [ ] microwave
- [ ] static oven
- [ ]

Preservation | temp. | time
- [ ] freezer
- [ ] fridge
- [ ] room temp.
- [ ]

container
- [ ] airtight container
- [ ] cling film
- [ ] food-grade bag
- [ ]

Notes

Picture

Memo

Recipes used
- Vol.
- Vol.
- Vol.
- Vol.

Recipe's variants
- Vol.
- Vol.

Recipe

Difficulty 🎩🎩🎩🎩🎩 Rating ☆☆☆☆☆   📅 Date ....

.... author ....

🚩 **Nationality** .... | 🧁 Dimensions .... | ⚖️ Weight .... | 🍪 Pieces .... | 👥 **Serves** ....

check ✓   🧂 **Ingredients**   ⚖️ Quantity (Q)   Percentage (%=Q:T×100)   🪙 Cost

🧁 **Type** of dessert
- [ ] basic recipe
- [ ] cake
- [ ] chocolate
- [ ] cookie
- [ ] fried
- [ ] leavened
- [ ] pastry
- [ ] pie
- [ ] tart
- [ ]

🎉 **Ideal for**
- [ ] breakfast
- [ ] dessert
- [ ] snacks
- [ ] occasion

🎂 **TOTAL** (Σ column values) .... (T) .... 100% ....

👥 **Per serving** (TOTAL : Serves)

- [ ]

❄️ **Seasonal**
- [ ] spring
- [ ] summer
- [ ] fall
- [ ] winter
- [ ] year round

🍴 **Utensils**

○ baking dish	○ grater	○ revolving cake stand
○ baking paper	○ kitchen scissors	○ rolling pin
○ baking tin	○ kitchen torch	○ rubber spatula
○ baking tray	○ knife	○ sieve
○ blender	○ ladle	○ skimmer
○ bowl	○ measuring cups set	○ soucepan
○ cake scraper	○ measuring spoons set	○ spoon
○ chopping board	○ mixer	○ squeezer
○ cling film	○ mold	○ strainer
○ cookie cutter	○ offset spatula	○ teaspoon
○ cooking pan	○ pasta roller	○ weight scale
○ cooling rack	○ pasta wheel	○ whisk
○ cup	○ pastry brush	○
○ digital thermometer	○ piping bag	○
○ dough mixer	○ piping nozzle	○
○ electric whisk	○ pot	○
○ fork	○ potato peeler	○

🍴 **Special diet**
- [ ] egg-free
- [ ] fat-free
- [ ] gluten-free
- [ ] lactose-free
- [ ] sugar-free
- [ ] vegan
- [ ] vegetarian
- [ ]

Instructions

Procedure | Time
- [ ] cooking
- [ ] cooling
- [ ] decorating
- [ ] freezing
- [ ] prepping
- [ ] proofing
- [ ] rest
- [ ]

TOT time

Cooking | temp. | time
- [ ] bain-marie
- [ ] cooktop
- [ ] fan oven
- [ ] fryer
- [ ] grill
- [ ] microwave
- [ ] static oven
- [ ]

Preservation | temp. | time
- [ ] freezer
- [ ] fridge
- [ ] room temp.
- [ ]

container
- [ ] airtight container
- [ ] cling film
- [ ] food-grade bag
- [ ]

Notes

Recipes used
- Vol.
- Vol.
- Vol.
- Vol.

Recipe's variants
- Vol.
- Vol.

Picture

Memo

Recipe

Difficulty ⊘⊘⊘⊘⊘ **Rating** ☆☆☆☆☆   📅 **Date** ....

.... *author* ....

🚩 **Nationality** .... 📺 **Dimensions** .... ⚖ **Weight** .... 🍪 **Pieces** .... 👥 **Serves** ....

🧁 **Type** of dessert
- [ ] basic recipe
- [ ] cake
- [ ] chocolate
- [ ] cookie
- [ ] fried
- [ ] leavened
- [ ] pastry
- [ ] pie
- [ ] tart
- [ ] ....

🎉 **Ideal for**
- [ ] breakfast
- [ ] dessert
- [ ] snacks
- [ ] occasion
- [ ] ....

❄ **Seasonal**
- [ ] spring
- [ ] summer
- [ ] fall
- [ ] winter
- [ ] year round

🍴 **Special diet**
- [ ] egg-free
- [ ] fat-free
- [ ] gluten-free
- [ ] lactose-free
- [ ] sugar-free
- [ ] vegan
- [ ] vegetarian
- [ ] ....

check	🍶 Ingredients	⚖ Quantity (Q)	Percentage (%=Q:T×100)	🪙 Cost
○				
○				
○				
○				
○				
○				
○				
○				
○				
○				
○				
○				
○				
○				

🎂 **TOTAL** (Σ column values) .... (T) .... 100% ....

👥 **Per serving** (TOTAL : Serves) ....

🍴 **Utensils**
- ○ baking dish
- ○ baking paper
- ○ baking tin
- ○ baking tray
- ○ blender
- ○ bowl
- ○ cake scraper
- ○ chopping board
- ○ cling film
- ○ cookie cutter
- ○ cooking pan
- ○ cooling rack
- ○ cup
- ○ digital thermometer
- ○ dough mixer
- ○ electric whisk
- ○ fork
- ○ grater
- ○ kitchen scissors
- ○ kitchen torch
- ○ knife
- ○ ladle
- ○ measuring cups set
- ○ measuring spoons set
- ○ mixer
- ○ mold
- ○ offset spatula
- ○ pasta roller
- ○ pasta wheel
- ○ pastry brush
- ○ piping bag
- ○ piping nozzle
- ○ pot
- ○ potato peeler
- ○ revolving cake stand
- ○ rolling pin
- ○ rubber spatula
- ○ sieve
- ○ skimmer
- ○ soucepan
- ○ spoon
- ○ squeezer
- ○ strainer
- ○ teaspoon
- ○ weight scale
- ○ whisk
- ○ ....
- ○ ....
- ○ ....

Instructions

Procedure | Time
- [ ] cooking
- [ ] cooling
- [ ] decorating
- [ ] freezing
- [ ] prepping
- [ ] proofing
- [ ] rest
- [ ]

TOT time

Cooking | temp. | time
- [ ] bain-marie
- [ ] cooktop
- [ ] fan oven
- [ ] fryer
- [ ] grill
- [ ] microwave
- [ ] static oven
- [ ]

Preservation | temp. | time
- [ ] freezer
- [ ] fridge
- [ ] room temp.
- [ ]

container
- [ ] airtight container
- [ ] cling film
- [ ] food-grade bag
- [ ]

Notes

Recipes used
- Vol.
- Vol.
- Vol.
- Vol.

Recipe's variants
- Vol.
- Vol.

Picture

Memo

Recipe

Difficulty ♕♕♕♕♕ Rating ☆☆☆☆☆   📅 Date _____

_____   author _____

🚩 **Nationality** _____   [🗄] Dimensions ____   [⚖] Weight ____   [🍪] Pieces ____   [👥] **Serves** ____

🧁 **Type** of dessert

- ☐ basic recipe
- ☐ cake
- ☐ chocolate
- ☐ cookie
- ☐ fried
- ☐ leavened
- ☐ pastry
- ☐ pie
- ☐ tart
- ☐ _____

check ✓

[🧂] **Ingredients**   [⚖] Quantity (Q)   Percentage (%=Q:T×100)   [💰] Cost

(ingredient rows)

🎉 **Ideal for**

- ☐ breakfast
- ☐ dessert
- ☐ snacks
- ☐ occasion
- ☐ _____

🎂 **TOTAL** (Σ column values) _____ (T) ____ 100%

👥 **Per serving** (TOTAL : Serves) _____

❄ **Seasonal**

- ☐ spring
- ☐ summer
- ☐ fall
- ☐ winter
- ☐ year round

🍴 **Utensils**

○ baking dish	○ grater	○ revolving cake stand
○ baking paper	○ kitchen scissors	○ rolling pin
○ baking tin	○ kitchen torch	○ rubber spatula
○ baking tray	○ knife	○ sieve
○ blender	○ ladle	○ skimmer
○ bowl	○ measuring cups set	○ soucepan
○ cake scraper	○ measuring spoons set	○ spoon
○ chopping board	○ mixer	○ squeezer
○ cling film	○ mold	○ strainer
○ cookie cutter	○ offset spatula	○ teaspoon
○ cooking pan	○ pasta roller	○ weight scale
○ cooling rack	○ pasta wheel	○ whisk
○ cup	○ pastry brush	○
○ digital thermometer	○ piping bag	○
○ dough mixer	○ piping nozzle	○
○ electric whisk	○ pot	○
○ fork	○ potato peeler	○

✳ **Special diet**

- ☐ egg-free
- ☐ fat-free
- ☐ gluten-free
- ☐ lactose-free
- ☐ sugar-free
- ☐ vegan
- ☐ vegetarian
- ☐ _____

Instructions

Procedure / Time
- [ ] cooking
- [ ] cooling
- [ ] decorating
- [ ] freezing
- [ ] prepping
- [ ] proofing
- [ ] rest
- [ ]

TOT time

Cooking — temp. / time
- [ ] bain-marie
- [ ] cooktop
- [ ] fan oven
- [ ] fryer
- [ ] grill
- [ ] microwave
- [ ] static oven
- [ ]

Preservation — temp. / time
- [ ] freezer
- [ ] fridge
- [ ] room temp.
- [ ]

container
- [ ] airtight container
- [ ] cling film
- [ ] food-grade bag
- [ ]

Notes

Recipes used
- Vol.
- Vol.
- Vol.
- Vol.

Recipe's variants
- Vol.
- Vol.

Picture

Memo

Recipe

Difficulty ♕♕♕♕♕ Rating ☆☆☆☆☆   📅 Date

author

🚩 Nationality   📦 Dimensions   ⚖ Weight   🍪 Pieces   👥 Serves

check

🧁 **Type** of dessert
- [ ] basic recipe
- [ ] cake
- [ ] chocolate
- [ ] cookie
- [ ] fried
- [ ] leavened
- [ ] pastry
- [ ] pie
- [ ] tart
- [ ]

🎉 **Ideal for**
- [ ] breakfast
- [ ] dessert
- [ ] snacks
- [ ] occasion
- [ ]

❄ **Seasonal**
- [ ] spring
- [ ] summer
- [ ] fall
- [ ] winter
- [ ] year round

🍴 **Special diet**
- [ ] egg-free
- [ ] fat-free
- [ ] gluten-free
- [ ] lactose-free
- [ ] sugar-free
- [ ] vegan
- [ ] vegetarian
- [ ]

🧂 **Ingredients** | Quantity (Q) | Percentage (%=Q:T×100) | Cost

🎂 TOTAL (Σ column values) (T)   100%

👥 Per serving (TOTAL : Serves)

🍴 **Utensils**
- ○ baking dish
- ○ baking paper
- ○ baking tin
- ○ baking tray
- ○ blender
- ○ bowl
- ○ cake scraper
- ○ chopping board
- ○ cling film
- ○ cookie cutter
- ○ cooking pan
- ○ cooling rack
- ○ cup
- ○ digital thermometer
- ○ dough mixer
- ○ electric whisk
- ○ fork
- ○ grater
- ○ kitchen scissors
- ○ kitchen torch
- ○ knife
- ○ ladle
- ○ measuring cups set
- ○ measuring spoons set
- ○ mixer
- ○ mold
- ○ offset spatula
- ○ pasta roller
- ○ pasta wheel
- ○ pastry brush
- ○ piping bag
- ○ piping nozzle
- ○ pot
- ○ potato peeler
- ○ revolving cake stand
- ○ rolling pin
- ○ rubber spatula
- ○ sieve
- ○ skimmer
- ○ soucepan
- ○ spoon
- ○ squeezer
- ○ strainer
- ○ teaspoon
- ○ weight scale
- ○ whisk
- ○
- ○
- ○

Instructions

Procedure | Time
- [ ] cooking
- [ ] cooling
- [ ] decorating
- [ ] freezing
- [ ] prepping
- [ ] proofing
- [ ] rest
- [ ]

TOT time

Cooking | temp. | time
- [ ] bain-marie
- [ ] cooktop
- [ ] fan oven
- [ ] fryer
- [ ] grill
- [ ] microwave
- [ ] static oven
- [ ]

Preservation | temp. | time
- [ ] freezer
- [ ] fridge
- [ ] room temp.
- [ ]

container
- [ ] airtight container
- [ ] cling film
- [ ] food-grade bag
- [ ]

Notes

Recipes used
- ◯ _____ Vol.
- ◯ _____ Vol.
- ◯ _____ Vol.
- ◯ _____ Vol.

Recipe's variants
- ◯ _____ Vol.
- ◯ _____ Vol.

Picture

Memo

Recipe

Difficulty 🎩🎩🎩🎩🎩 **Rating** ☆☆☆☆☆ 📅 **Date**

author

🚩 **Nationality** | 📷 Dimensions | ⚖ Weight | 🍪 Pieces | 👥 **Serves**

🧁 **Type** of dessert
- ☐ basic recipe
- ☐ cake
- ☐ chocolate
- ☐ cookie
- ☐ fried
- ☐ leavened
- ☐ pastry
- ☐ pie
- ☐ tart
- ☐

check ✓ 🧂 **Ingredients**   ⏲ Quantity (Q)   Percentage (%=Q:T×100)   💰 Cost

🎉 **Ideal for**
- ☐ breakfast
- ☐ dessert
- ☐ snacks
- ☐ occasion
- ☐

🎂 **TOTAL** (Σ column values)   (T)   100%
👥 **Per serving** (TOTAL : Serves)

❄ **Seasonal**
- ☐ spring
- ☐ summer
- ☐ fall
- ☐ winter
- ☐ year round

🍴 **Utensils**

○ baking dish	○ grater	○ revolving cake stand
○ baking paper	○ kitchen scissors	○ rolling pin
○ baking tin	○ kitchen torch	○ rubber spatula
○ baking tray	○ knife	○ sieve
○ blender	○ ladle	○ skimmer
○ bowl	○ measuring cups set	○ soucepan
○ cake scraper	○ measuring spoons set	○ spoon
○ chopping board	○ mixer	○ squeezer
○ cling film	○ mold	○ strainer
○ cookie cutter	○ offset spatula	○ teaspoon
○ cooking pan	○ pasta roller	○ weight scale
○ cooling rack	○ pasta wheel	○ whisk
○ cup	○ pastry brush	○
○ digital thermometer	○ piping bag	○
○ dough mixer	○ piping nozzle	○
○ electric whisk	○ pot	○
○ fork	○ potato peeler	○

🍴 **Special diet**
- ☐ egg-free
- ☐ fat-free
- ☐ gluten-free
- ☐ lactose-free
- ☐ sugar-free
- ☐ vegan
- ☐ vegetarian
- ☐

Instructions

Procedure | Time
- [ ] cooking
- [ ] cooling
- [ ] decorating
- [ ] freezing
- [ ] prepping
- [ ] proofing
- [ ] rest
- [ ]

TOT time

Cooking | temp. | time
- [ ] bain-marie
- [ ] cooktop
- [ ] fan oven
- [ ] fryer
- [ ] grill
- [ ] microwave
- [ ] static oven
- [ ]

Preservation | temp. | time
- [ ] freezer
- [ ] fridge
- [ ] room temp.
- [ ]

container
- [ ] airtight container
- [ ] cling film
- [ ] food-grade bag
- [ ]

Notes

Recipes used
- Vol.
- Vol.
- Vol.
- Vol.

Recipe's variants
- Vol.
- Vol.

Picture

Memo

Recipe

Difficulty ☐☐☐☐☐ **Rating** ☆☆☆☆☆   📅 **Date** ....

....   author ....

🚩 **Nationality** ....   📺 Dimensions .... ⚖ Weight .... 🍪 Pieces .... 👥 **Serves** ....

check ✓

🧁 **Type** of dessert
- ☐ basic recipe
- ☐ cake
- ☐ chocolate
- ☐ cookie
- ☐ fried
- ☐ leavened
- ☐ pastry
- ☐ pie
- ☐ tart
- ☐ ....

🎉 **Ideal for**
- ☐ breakfast
- ☐ dessert
- ☐ snacks
- ☐ occasion
- ☐ ....

❄ **Seasonal**
- ☐ spring
- ☐ summer
- ☐ fall
- ☐ winter
- ☐ year round

🍴 **Special diet**
- ☐ egg-free
- ☐ fat-free
- ☐ gluten-free
- ☐ lactose-free
- ☐ sugar-free
- ☐ vegan
- ☐ vegetarian

🧂 **Ingredients** ⏱ Quantity (Q) Percentage (%=Q:T×100) 💰 Cost

(ingredient lines)

🎂 **TOTAL** (Σ column values) .... (T) 100%
👥 **Per serving** (TOTAL : Serves) ....

🍴 **Utensils**
- ○ baking dish
- ○ baking paper
- ○ baking tin
- ○ baking tray
- ○ blender
- ○ bowl
- ○ cake scraper
- ○ chopping board
- ○ cling film
- ○ cookie cutter
- ○ cooking pan
- ○ cooling rack
- ○ cup
- ○ digital thermometer
- ○ dough mixer
- ○ electric whisk
- ○ fork
- ○ grater
- ○ kitchen scissors
- ○ kitchen torch
- ○ knife
- ○ ladle
- ○ measuring cups set
- ○ measuring spoons set
- ○ mixer
- ○ mold
- ○ offset spatula
- ○ pasta roller
- ○ pasta wheel
- ○ pastry brush
- ○ piping bag
- ○ piping nozzle
- ○ pot
- ○ potato peeler
- ○ revolving cake stand
- ○ rolling pin
- ○ rubber spatula
- ○ sieve
- ○ skimmer
- ○ soucepan
- ○ spoon
- ○ squeezer
- ○ strainer
- ○ teaspoon
- ○ weight scale
- ○ whisk
- ○ ....
- ○ ....
- ○ ....
- ○ ....

Instructions

Procedure | Time
- [ ] cooking
- [ ] cooling
- [ ] decorating
- [ ] freezing
- [ ] prepping
- [ ] proofing
- [ ] rest
- [ ]

TOT time

Cooking — temp. | time
- [ ] bain-marie
- [ ] cooktop
- [ ] fan oven
- [ ] fryer
- [ ] grill
- [ ] microwave
- [ ] static oven
- [ ]

Preservation — temp. | time
- [ ] freezer
- [ ] fridge
- [ ] room temp.
- [ ]

container
- [ ] airtight container
- [ ] cling film
- [ ] food-grade bag
- [ ]

Notes

Picture

Memo

Recipes used
- Vol.
- Vol.
- Vol.
- Vol.

Recipe's variants
- Vol.
- Vol.

Recipe

Difficulty ♧♧♧♧♧ Rating ☆☆☆☆☆   📅 Date

author

🚩 Nationality   📦 Dimensions   ⚖ Weight   🍪 Pieces   👥 Serves

check	🧂 Ingredients	⏲ Quantity (Q)	Percentage (%=Q:T×100)	🪙 Cost

🧁 **Type** of dessert
- ☐ basic recipe
- ☐ cake
- ☐ chocolate
- ☐ cookie
- ☐ fried
- ☐ leavened
- ☐ pastry
- ☐ pie
- ☐ tart
- ☐

🎉 **Ideal for**
- ☐ breakfast
- ☐ dessert
- ☐ snacks
- ☐ occasion
- ☐

🎂 TOTAL (Σ column values) (T) 100%

👥 Per serving (TOTAL : Serves)

❄ **Seasonal**
- ☐ spring
- ☐ summer
- ☐ fall
- ☐ winter
- ☐ year round

🍴 **Utensils**
○ baking dish	○ grater	○ revolving cake stand
○ baking paper	○ kitchen scissors	○ rolling pin
○ baking tin	○ kitchen torch	○ rubber spatula
○ baking tray	○ knife	○ sieve
○ blender	○ ladle	○ skimmer
○ bowl	○ measuring cups set	○ soucepan
○ cake scraper	○ measuring spoons set	○ spoon
○ chopping board	○ mixer	○ squeezer
○ cling film	○ mold	○ strainer
○ cookie cutter	○ offset spatula	○ teaspoon
○ cooking pan	○ pasta roller	○ weight scale
○ cooling rack	○ pasta wheel	○ whisk
○ cup	○ pastry brush	○
○ digital thermometer	○ piping bag	○
○ dough mixer	○ piping nozzle	○
○ electric whisk	○ pot	○
○ fork	○ potato peeler	○

✘ **Special diet**
- ☐ egg-free
- ☐ fat-free
- ☐ gluten-free
- ☐ lactose-free
- ☐ sugar-free
- ☐ vegan
- ☐ vegetarian
- ☐

Instructions

Procedure | Time
- [ ] cooking
- [ ] cooling
- [ ] decorating
- [ ] freezing
- [ ] prepping
- [ ] proofing
- [ ] rest
- [ ]

TOT time

Cooking | temp. | time
- [ ] bain-marie
- [ ] cooktop
- [ ] fan oven
- [ ] fryer
- [ ] grill
- [ ] microwave
- [ ] static oven
- [ ]

Preservation | temp. | time
- [ ] freezer
- [ ] fridge
- [ ] room temp.
- [ ]

container
- [ ] airtight container
- [ ] cling film
- [ ] food-grade bag
- [ ]

Notes

Picture

Memo

Recipes used
- Vol.
- Vol.
- Vol.
- Vol.

Recipe's variants
- Vol.
- Vol.

Recipe

Difficulty ♡♡♡♡♡ **Rating** ☆☆☆☆☆   📅 **Date** ....

....   author ....

🏳 **Nationality** ....   📺 Dimensions ....   ⚖ Weight ....   🍪 Pieces ....   👥 **Serves** ....

🧁 **Type** of dessert

- [ ] basic recipe
- [ ] cake
- [ ] chocolate
- [ ] cookie
- [ ] fried
- [ ] leavened
- [ ] pastry
- [ ] pie
- [ ] tart
- [ ] ....

🎉 **Ideal for**

- [ ] breakfast
- [ ] dessert
- [ ] snacks
- [ ] occasion
- [ ] ....

❄ **Seasonal**

- [ ] spring
- [ ] summer
- [ ] fall
- [ ] winter
- [ ] year round

✽ **Special diet**

- [ ] egg-free
- [ ] fat-free
- [ ] gluten-free
- [ ] lactose-free
- [ ] sugar-free
- [ ] vegan
- [ ] vegetarian
- [ ] ....

check	🥫 **Ingredients**	⏲ Quantity (Q)	Percentage (%=Q:T×100)	🪙 Cost	
○					
○					
○					
○					
○					
○					
○					
○					
○					
○					
○					
○					

🎂 **TOTAL** (Σ column values) .... (T)............. 100%

👥 **Per serving** (TOTAL : Serves) ....

🍴 **Utensils**

○ baking dish	○ grater	○ revolving cake stand
○ baking paper	○ kitchen scissors	○ rolling pin
○ baking tin	○ kitchen torch	○ rubber spatula
○ baking tray	○ knife	○ sieve
○ blender	○ ladle	○ skimmer
○ bowl	○ measuring cups set	○ soucepan
○ cake scraper	○ measuring spoons set	○ spoon
○ chopping board	○ mixer	○ squeezer
○ cling film	○ mold	○ strainer
○ cookie cutter	○ offset spatula	○ teaspoon
○ cooking pan	○ pasta roller	○ weight scale
○ cooling rack	○ pasta wheel	○ whisk
○ cup	○ pastry brush	○
○ digital thermometer	○ piping bag	○
○ dough mixer	○ piping nozzle	○
○ electric whisk	○ pot	○
○ fork	○ potato peeler	○

Instructions

Procedure / Time
- [ ] cooking
- [ ] cooling
- [ ] decorating
- [ ] freezing
- [ ] prepping
- [ ] proofing
- [ ] rest
- [ ]

TOT time

Cooking / temp. / time
- [ ] bain-marie
- [ ] cooktop
- [ ] fan oven
- [ ] fryer
- [ ] grill
- [ ] microwave
- [ ] static oven
- [ ]

Preservation / temp. / time
- [ ] freezer
- [ ] fridge
- [ ] room temp.
- [ ]

container
- [ ] airtight container
- [ ] cling film
- [ ] food-grade bag
- [ ]

Notes

Recipes used
- Vol.
- Vol.
- Vol.
- Vol.

Recipe's variants
- Vol.
- Vol.

Picture

Memo

Recipe

Difficulty ⌒⌒⌒⌒⌒ **Rating** ☆☆☆☆☆ 📅 **Date** _____

_____ author _____

🚩 **Nationality** ____ | 📦 Dimensions ____ | ⚖ Weight ____ | 🍪 Pieces ____ | 👥 **Serves** ____

🧁 Type of dessert
- [ ] basic recipe
- [ ] cake
- [ ] chocolate
- [ ] cookie
- [ ] fried
- [ ] leavened
- [ ] pastry
- [ ] pie
- [ ] tart
- [ ] ____

🎉 Ideal for
- [ ] breakfast
- [ ] dessert
- [ ] snacks
- [ ] occasion
- [ ] ____

❄ Seasonal
- [ ] spring
- [ ] summer
- [ ] fall
- [ ] winter
- [ ] year round

🍴 Special diet
- [ ] egg-free
- [ ] fat-free
- [ ] gluten-free
- [ ] lactose-free
- [ ] sugar-free
- [ ] vegan
- [ ] vegetarian
- [ ] ____

🧂 Ingredients | check | Quantity (Q) | Percentage (%=Q:T×100) | 💰 Cost

check	Ingredient	Quantity (Q)	Percentage	Cost
○				
○				
○				
○				
○				
○				
○				
○				
○				
○				
○				
○				
○				
○				

🎂 **TOTAL** (Σ column values) ____ (T) ____ 100% ____

👥 **Per serving** (TOTAL : Serves) ____

🍴 Utensils

- ○ baking dish
- ○ baking paper
- ○ baking tin
- ○ baking tray
- ○ blender
- ○ bowl
- ○ cake scraper
- ○ chopping board
- ○ cling film
- ○ cookie cutter
- ○ cooking pan
- ○ cooling rack
- ○ cup
- ○ digital thermometer
- ○ dough mixer
- ○ electric whisk
- ○ fork
- ○ grater
- ○ kitchen scissors
- ○ kitchen torch
- ○ knife
- ○ ladle
- ○ measuring cups set
- ○ measuring spoons set
- ○ mixer
- ○ mold
- ○ offset spatula
- ○ pasta roller
- ○ pasta wheel
- ○ pastry brush
- ○ piping bag
- ○ piping nozzle
- ○ pot
- ○ potato peeler
- ○ revolving cake stand
- ○ rolling pin
- ○ rubber spatula
- ○ sieve
- ○ skimmer
- ○ soucepan
- ○ spoon
- ○ squeezer
- ○ strainer
- ○ teaspoon
- ○ weight scale
- ○ whisk
- ○ ____
- ○ ____
- ○ ____

Instructions

Procedure | Time
- [ ] cooking
- [ ] cooling
- [ ] decorating
- [ ] freezing
- [ ] prepping
- [ ] proofing
- [ ] rest
- [ ]

TOT time

Cooking | temp. | time
- [ ] bain-marie
- [ ] cooktop
- [ ] fan oven
- [ ] fryer
- [ ] grill
- [ ] microwave
- [ ] static oven
- [ ]

Preservation | temp. | time
- [ ] freezer
- [ ] fridge
- [ ] room temp.
- [ ]

container
- [ ] airtight container
- [ ] cling film
- [ ] food-grade bag
- [ ]

Recipes used
- Vol.
- Vol.
- Vol.
- Vol.

Recipe's variants
- Vol.
- Vol.

Notes

Picture

Memo

Recipe

Difficulty ☐☐☐☐☐   Rating ☆☆☆☆☆   📅 Date _____

_____   author _____

🚩 **Nationality** _____   📦 Dimensions _____   ⚖ Weight _____   🍪 Pieces _____   👥 **Serves** _____

🧁 **Type** of dessert
- ☐ basic recipe
- ☐ cake
- ☐ chocolate
- ☐ cookie
- ☐ fried
- ☐ leavened
- ☐ pastry
- ☐ pie
- ☐ tart
- ☐ _____

🎉 **Ideal for**
- ☐ breakfast
- ☐ dessert
- ☐ snacks
- ☐ occasion
- ☐ _____

❄ **Seasonal**
- ☐ spring
- ☐ summer
- ☐ fall
- ☐ winter
- ☐ year round

✖ **Special diet**
- ☐ egg-free
- ☐ fat-free
- ☐ gluten-free
- ☐ lactose-free
- ☐ sugar-free
- ☐ vegan
- ☐ vegetarian
- ☐ _____

check ✓	🧂 Ingredients	Quantity (Q)	Percentage (%=Q:T×100)	💰 Cost
○				
○				
○				
○				
○				
○				
○				
○				
○				
○				
○				
○				
○				
○				

🎂 **TOTAL** (Σ column values) _____ (T) _____ 100% _____

👥 **Per serving** (TOTAL : Serves) _____

🍴 **Utensils**

- ○ baking dish
- ○ baking paper
- ○ baking tin
- ○ baking tray
- ○ blender
- ○ bowl
- ○ cake scraper
- ○ chopping board
- ○ cling film
- ○ cookie cutter
- ○ cooking pan
- ○ cooling rack
- ○ cup
- ○ digital thermometer
- ○ dough mixer
- ○ electric whisk
- ○ fork

- ○ grater
- ○ kitchen scissors
- ○ kitchen torch
- ○ knife
- ○ ladle
- ○ measuring cups set
- ○ measuring spoons set
- ○ mixer
- ○ mold
- ○ offset spatula
- ○ pasta roller
- ○ pasta wheel
- ○ pastry brush
- ○ piping bag
- ○ piping nozzle
- ○ pot
- ○ potato peeler

- ○ revolving cake stand
- ○ rolling pin
- ○ rubber spatula
- ○ sieve
- ○ skimmer
- ○ soucepan
- ○ spoon
- ○ squeezer
- ○ strainer
- ○ teaspoon
- ○ weight scale
- ○ whisk
- ○
- ○
- ○

Instructions

Procedure — Time
- [ ] cooking
- [ ] cooling
- [ ] decorating
- [ ] freezing
- [ ] prepping
- [ ] proofing
- [ ] rest
- [ ]

TOT time

Cooking — temp. — time
- [ ] bain-marie
- [ ] cooktop
- [ ] fan oven
- [ ] fryer
- [ ] grill
- [ ] microwave
- [ ] static oven
- [ ]

Preservation — temp. — time
- [ ] freezer
- [ ] fridge
- [ ] room temp.
- [ ]

container
- [ ] airtight container
- [ ] cling film
- [ ] food-grade bag
- [ ]

Notes

Picture

Memo

Recipes used
- Vol.
- Vol.
- Vol.
- Vol.

Recipe's variants
- Vol.
- Vol.

Recipe

Difficulty ♛♛♛♛♛ Rating ☆☆☆☆☆   📅 Date ....

....   author ....

🚩 Nationality .... 🍰 Dimensions .... ⚖ Weight .... 🍪 Pieces .... 👥 Serves ....

🧁 Type of dessert
- ☐ basic recipe
- ☐ cake
- ☐ chocolate
- ☐ cookie
- ☐ fried
- ☐ leavened
- ☐ pastry
- ☐ pie
- ☐ tart
- ☐ ....

🎉 Ideal for
- ☐ breakfast
- ☐ dessert
- ☐ snacks
- ☐ occasion
- ☐ ....

❄ Seasonal
- ☐ spring
- ☐ summer
- ☐ fall
- ☐ winter
- ☐ year round

🍴 Special diet
- ☐ egg-free
- ☐ fat-free
- ☐ gluten-free
- ☐ lactose-free
- ☐ sugar-free
- ☐ vegan
- ☐ vegetarian
- ☐ ....

check	🧂 Ingredients	⚖ Quantity (Q)	Percentage (%=Q:T×100)	🪙 Cost
○				
○				
○				
○				
○				
○				
○				
○				
○				
○				
○				
○				
○				

🎂 **TOTAL** (Σ column values) .... (T) 100%

👥 **Per serving** (TOTAL : Serves) ....

🍴 Utensils
- ○ baking dish
- ○ baking paper
- ○ baking tin
- ○ baking tray
- ○ blender
- ○ bowl
- ○ cake scraper
- ○ chopping board
- ○ cling film
- ○ cookie cutter
- ○ cooking pan
- ○ cooling rack
- ○ cup
- ○ digital thermometer
- ○ dough mixer
- ○ electric whisk
- ○ fork
- ○ grater
- ○ kitchen scissors
- ○ kitchen torch
- ○ knife
- ○ ladle
- ○ measuring cups set
- ○ measuring spoons set
- ○ mixer
- ○ mold
- ○ offset spatula
- ○ pasta roller
- ○ pasta wheel
- ○ pastry brush
- ○ piping bag
- ○ piping nozzle
- ○ pot
- ○ potato peeler
- ○ revolving cake stand
- ○ rolling pin
- ○ rubber spatula
- ○ sieve
- ○ skimmer
- ○ soucepan
- ○ spoon
- ○ squeezer
- ○ strainer
- ○ teaspoon
- ○ weight scale
- ○ whisk
- ○ ....
- ○ ....
- ○ ....
- ○ ....

Instructions

Procedure / Time
- [ ] cooking
- [ ] cooling
- [ ] decorating
- [ ] freezing
- [ ] prepping
- [ ] proofing
- [ ] rest
- [ ]

TOT time

Cooking — temp. / time
- [ ] bain-marie
- [ ] cooktop
- [ ] fan oven
- [ ] fryer
- [ ] grill
- [ ] microwave
- [ ] static oven
- [ ]

Preservation — temp. / time
- [ ] freezer
- [ ] fridge
- [ ] room temp.
- [ ]

container
- [ ] airtight container
- [ ] cling film
- [ ] food-grade bag
- [ ]

Notes

Recipes used
- Vol.
- Vol.
- Vol.
- Vol.

Recipe's variants
- Vol.
- Vol.

Picture

Memo

Recipe

Difficulty ▢▢▢▢▢ Rating ☆☆☆☆☆ 📅 Date _____

_____ author _____

🚩 **Nationality** _____ 🍰 Dimensions _____ ⚖️ Weight _____ 🍪 Pieces _____ 👥 Serves _____

🧁 **Type** of dessert
- ☐ basic recipe
- ☐ cake
- ☐ chocolate
- ☐ cookie
- ☐ fried
- ☐ leavened
- ☐ pastry
- ☐ pie
- ☐ tart
- ☐ _____

🎉 **Ideal for**
- ☐ breakfast
- ☐ dessert
- ☐ snacks
- ☐ occasion
- ☐ _____

❄️ **Seasonal**
- ☐ spring
- ☐ summer
- ☐ fall
- ☐ winter
- ☐ year round

✴️ **Special diet**
- ☐ egg-free
- ☐ fat-free
- ☐ gluten-free
- ☐ lactose-free
- ☐ sugar-free
- ☐ vegan
- ☐ vegetarian
- ☐ _____

check ✓

🧂 **Ingredients** | Quantity (Q) | Percentage (%=Q:T×100) | 💰 Cost

(blank rows for entries)

🎂 **TOTAL** (Σ column values)   (T) _____   100%
👥 **Per serving** (TOTAL : Serves)

🍴 **Utensils**

- ○ baking dish
- ○ baking paper
- ○ baking tin
- ○ baking tray
- ○ blender
- ○ bowl
- ○ cake scraper
- ○ chopping board
- ○ cling film
- ○ cookie cutter
- ○ cooking pan
- ○ cooling rack
- ○ cup
- ○ digital thermometer
- ○ dough mixer
- ○ electric whisk
- ○ fork

- ○ grater
- ○ kitchen scissors
- ○ kitchen torch
- ○ knife
- ○ ladle
- ○ measuring cups set
- ○ measuring spoons set
- ○ mixer
- ○ mold
- ○ offset spatula
- ○ pasta roller
- ○ pasta wheel
- ○ pastry brush
- ○ piping bag
- ○ piping nozzle
- ○ pot
- ○ potato peeler

- ○ revolving cake stand
- ○ rolling pin
- ○ rubber spatula
- ○ sieve
- ○ skimmer
- ○ soucepan
- ○ spoon
- ○ squeezer
- ○ strainer
- ○ teaspoon
- ○ weight scale
- ○ whisk
- ○ _____
- ○ _____
- ○ _____

Instructions

Procedure | Time
- [ ] cooking
- [ ] cooling
- [ ] decorating
- [ ] freezing
- [ ] prepping
- [ ] proofing
- [ ] rest
- [ ]

TOT time

Cooking | temp. | time
- [ ] bain-marie
- [ ] cooktop
- [ ] fan oven
- [ ] fryer
- [ ] grill
- [ ] microwave
- [ ] static oven
- [ ]

Preservation | temp. | time
- [ ] freezer
- [ ] fridge
- [ ] room temp.
- [ ]

container
- [ ] airtight container
- [ ] cling film
- [ ] food-grade bag
- [ ]

Notes

Picture

Memo

Recipes used
- Vol.
- Vol.
- Vol.
- Vol.

Recipe's variants
- Vol.
- Vol.

Recipe

Difficulty ☐☐☐☐☐   Rating ☆☆☆☆☆   📅 Date _____

_____   author _____

🚩 Nationality   🎂 Dimensions   ⚖ Weight   🍪 Pieces   👥 Serves

🧁 Type of dessert
- ☐ basic recipe
- ☐ cake
- ☐ chocolate
- ☐ cookie
- ☐ fried
- ☐ leavened
- ☐ pastry
- ☐ pie
- ☐ tart
- ☐ _____

🎉 Ideal for
- ☐ breakfast
- ☐ dessert
- ☐ snacks
- ☐ occasion
- ☐ _____

❄ Seasonal
- ☐ spring
- ☐ summer
- ☐ fall
- ☐ winter
- ☐ year round

✖ Special diet
- ☐ egg-free
- ☐ fat-free
- ☐ gluten-free
- ☐ lactose-free
- ☐ sugar-free
- ☐ vegan
- ☐ vegetarian
- ☐ _____

check ✓ 🫙 Ingredients   ⚖ Quantity (Q) | Percentage (%=Q:T×100) | 🪙 Cost

○ ....
○ ....
○ ....
○ ....
○ ....
○ ....
○ ....
○ ....
○ ....
○ ....
○ ....
○ ....
○ ....

🎂 **TOTAL** (Σ column values)   (T) 100%

👥 **Per serving** (TOTAL : Serves)

🍴 Utensils
- ○ baking dish
- ○ baking paper
- ○ baking tin
- ○ baking tray
- ○ blender
- ○ bowl
- ○ cake scraper
- ○ chopping board
- ○ cling film
- ○ cookie cutter
- ○ cooking pan
- ○ cooling rack
- ○ cup
- ○ digital thermometer
- ○ dough mixer
- ○ electric whisk
- ○ fork
- ○ grater
- ○ kitchen scissors
- ○ kitchen torch
- ○ knife
- ○ ladle
- ○ measuring cups set
- ○ measuring spoons set
- ○ mixer
- ○ mold
- ○ offset spatula
- ○ pasta roller
- ○ pasta wheel
- ○ pastry brush
- ○ piping bag
- ○ piping nozzle
- ○ pot
- ○ potato peeler
- ○ revolving cake stand
- ○ rolling pin
- ○ rubber spatula
- ○ sieve
- ○ skimmer
- ○ soucepan
- ○ spoon
- ○ squeezer
- ○ strainer
- ○ teaspoon
- ○ weight scale
- ○ whisk
- ○ _____
- ○ _____
- ○ _____

Instructions

Procedure | Time
- [ ] cooking
- [ ] cooling
- [ ] decorating
- [ ] freezing
- [ ] prepping
- [ ] proofing
- [ ] rest
- [ ]

TOT time

Cooking | temp. | time
- [ ] bain-marie
- [ ] cooktop
- [ ] fan oven
- [ ] fryer
- [ ] grill
- [ ] microwave
- [ ] static oven
- [ ]

Preservation | temp. | time
- [ ] freezer
- [ ] fridge
- [ ] room temp.
- [ ]

container
- [ ] airtight container
- [ ] cling film
- [ ] food-grade bag
- [ ]

Notes

Recipes used
- Vol.
- Vol.
- Vol.
- Vol.

Recipe's variants
- Vol.
- Vol.

Picture

Memo

Recipe

Difficulty ☷☷☷☷☷ **Rating** ☆☆☆☆☆   📅 **Date** ....

....

author ....

🚩 **Nationality** .... 📺 Dimensions ⚖️ Weight 🍪 Pieces 👥 **Serves**

🧁 **Type** of dessert
- [ ] basic recipe
- [ ] cake
- [ ] chocolate
- [ ] cookie
- [ ] fried
- [ ] leavened
- [ ] pastry
- [ ] pie
- [ ] tart
- [ ] ....

🎉 **Ideal for**
- [ ] breakfast
- [ ] dessert
- [ ] snacks
- [ ] occasion
- [ ] ....

❄️ **Seasonal**
- [ ] spring
- [ ] summer
- [ ] fall
- [ ] winter
- [ ] year round

🍴 **Special diet**
- [ ] egg-free
- [ ] fat-free
- [ ] gluten-free
- [ ] lactose-free
- [ ] sugar-free
- [ ] vegan
- [ ] vegetarian
- [ ] ....

check ✓

🥫 **Ingredients**   ⏲️ Quantity (Q)   Percentage (%=Q:T×100)   🪙 Cost

🎂 **TOTAL** (Σ column values) .... (T) .... 100% ....

👥 **Per serving** (TOTAL : Serves) ....

🍴 **Utensils**
- ○ baking dish
- ○ baking paper
- ○ baking tin
- ○ baking tray
- ○ blender
- ○ bowl
- ○ cake scraper
- ○ chopping board
- ○ cling film
- ○ cookie cutter
- ○ cooking pan
- ○ cooling rack
- ○ cup
- ○ digital thermometer
- ○ dough mixer
- ○ electric whisk
- ○ fork
- ○ grater
- ○ kitchen scissors
- ○ kitchen torch
- ○ knife
- ○ ladle
- ○ measuring cups set
- ○ measuring spoons set
- ○ mixer
- ○ mold
- ○ offset spatula
- ○ pasta roller
- ○ pasta wheel
- ○ pastry brush
- ○ piping bag
- ○ piping nozzle
- ○ pot
- ○ potato peeler
- ○ revolving cake stand
- ○ rolling pin
- ○ rubber spatula
- ○ sieve
- ○ skimmer
- ○ soucepan
- ○ spoon
- ○ squeezer
- ○ strainer
- ○ teaspoon
- ○ weight scale
- ○ whisk
- ○ ....
- ○ ....

Instructions

Notes

Picture

Memo

Procedure | Time
- [ ] cooking
- [ ] cooling
- [ ] decorating
- [ ] freezing
- [ ] prepping
- [ ] proofing
- [ ] rest
- [ ]

TOT time

Cooking | temp. | time
- [ ] bain-marie
- [ ] cooktop
- [ ] fan oven
- [ ] fryer
- [ ] grill
- [ ] microwave
- [ ] static oven
- [ ]

Preservation | temp. | time
- [ ] freezer
- [ ] fridge
- [ ] room temp.
- [ ]

container
- [ ] airtight container
- [ ] cling film
- [ ] food-grade bag
- [ ]

Recipes used
Vol.
Vol.
Vol.
Vol.

Recipe's variants
Vol.
Vol.

Recipe

Difficulty ☐☐☐☐☐   **Rating** ☆☆☆☆☆   📅 Date ....

....   author ....

🚩 Nationality ....   📺 Dimensions ....   ⚖️ Weight ....   🍪 Pieces ....   👣 **Serves** ....

🧁 Type of dessert
- ☐ basic recipe
- ☐ cake
- ☐ chocolate
- ☐ cookie
- ☐ fried
- ☐ leavened
- ☐ pastry
- ☐ pie
- ☐ tart
- ☐ ....

🎉 Ideal for
- ☐ breakfast
- ☐ dessert
- ☐ snacks
- ☐ occasion
- ☐ ....

❄️ Seasonal
- ☐ spring
- ☐ summer
- ☐ fall
- ☐ winter
- ☐ year round

🍴 Special diet
- ☐ egg-free
- ☐ fat-free
- ☐ gluten-free
- ☐ lactose-free
- ☐ sugar-free
- ☐ vegan
- ☐ vegetarian
- ☐ ....

check ✓

🫙 Ingredients | ⏲️ Quantity (Q) | Percentage (%=Q:T×100) | 🪙 Cost

(lines for ingredients)

🎂 **TOTAL** (Σ column values) .... (T) 100%

👣 **Per serving** (TOTAL : Serves) ....

🍴 Utensils
- ○ baking dish
- ○ baking paper
- ○ baking tin
- ○ baking tray
- ○ blender
- ○ bowl
- ○ cake scraper
- ○ chopping board
- ○ cling film
- ○ cookie cutter
- ○ cooking pan
- ○ cooling rack
- ○ cup
- ○ digital thermometer
- ○ dough mixer
- ○ electric whisk
- ○ fork

- ○ grater
- ○ kitchen scissors
- ○ kitchen torch
- ○ knife
- ○ ladle
- ○ measuring cups set
- ○ measuring spoons set
- ○ mixer
- ○ mold
- ○ offset spatula
- ○ pasta roller
- ○ pasta wheel
- ○ pastry brush
- ○ piping bag
- ○ piping nozzle
- ○ pot
- ○ potato peeler

- ○ revolving cake stand
- ○ rolling pin
- ○ rubber spatula
- ○ sieve
- ○ skimmer
- ○ soucepan
- ○ spoon
- ○ squeezer
- ○ strainer
- ○ teaspoon
- ○ weight scale
- ○ whisk
- ○ ....
- ○ ....
- ○ ....
- ○ ....

Instructions

Procedure | Time
- [ ] cooking
- [ ] cooling
- [ ] decorating
- [ ] freezing
- [ ] prepping
- [ ] proofing
- [ ] rest
- [ ]

TOT time

Cooking | temp. | time
- [ ] bain-marie
- [ ] cooktop
- [ ] fan oven
- [ ] fryer
- [ ] grill
- [ ] microwave
- [ ] static oven
- [ ]

Preservation | temp. | time
- [ ] freezer
- [ ] fridge
- [ ] room temp.
- [ ]

container
- [ ] airtight container
- [ ] cling film
- [ ] food-grade bag
- [ ]

Notes

Recipes used
- Vol.
- Vol.
- Vol.
- Vol.

Recipe's variants
- Vol.
- Vol.

Picture

Memo

Recipe

Difficulty ♢♢♢♢♢ **Rating** ☆☆☆☆☆   📅 **Date** ....

....   author ....

🚩 **Nationality** ....   📦 Dimensions ....   ⚖ Weight ....   🍪 Pieces ....   👥 **Serves** ....

🧁 **Type** of dessert

- ☐ basic recipe
- ☐ cake
- ☐ chocolate
- ☐ cookie
- ☐ fried
- ☐ leavened
- ☐ pastry
- ☐ pie
- ☐ tart
- ☐ ....

🎉 **Ideal for**

- ☐ breakfast
- ☐ dessert
- ☐ snacks
- ☐ occasion
- ☐ ....

❄ **Seasonal**

- ☐ spring
- ☐ summer
- ☐ fall
- ☐ winter
- ☐ year round

🍴 **Special diet**

- ☐ egg-free
- ☐ fat-free
- ☐ gluten-free
- ☐ lactose-free
- ☐ sugar-free
- ☐ vegan
- ☐ vegetarian
- ☐ ....

check	🫙 **Ingredients**	⚖ Quantity (Q)	Percentage (%=Q:T×100)	🪙 Cost
○				
○				
○				
○				
○				
○				
○				
○				
○				
○				
○				
○				
○				
○				

🎂 **TOTAL** (Σ column values) .... (T).......... 100%

👥 **Per serving** (TOTAL : Serves) ....

🍴 **Utensils**

- ○ baking dish
- ○ baking paper
- ○ baking tin
- ○ baking tray
- ○ blender
- ○ bowl
- ○ cake scraper
- ○ chopping board
- ○ cling film
- ○ cookie cutter
- ○ cooking pan
- ○ cooling rack
- ○ cup
- ○ digital thermometer
- ○ dough mixer
- ○ electric whisk
- ○ fork
- ○ grater
- ○ kitchen scissors
- ○ kitchen torch
- ○ knife
- ○ ladle
- ○ measuring cups set
- ○ measuring spoons set
- ○ mixer
- ○ mold
- ○ offset spatula
- ○ pasta roller
- ○ pasta wheel
- ○ pastry brush
- ○ piping bag
- ○ piping nozzle
- ○ pot
- ○ potato peeler
- ○ revolving cake stand
- ○ rolling pin
- ○ rubber spatula
- ○ sieve
- ○ skimmer
- ○ soucepan
- ○ spoon
- ○ squeezer
- ○ strainer
- ○ teaspoon
- ○ weight scale
- ○ whisk

Instructions

Procedure / Time
- [ ] cooking
- [ ] cooling
- [ ] decorating
- [ ] freezing
- [ ] prepping
- [ ] proofing
- [ ] rest
- [ ]

TOT time

Cooking — temp. / time
- [ ] bain-marie
- [ ] cooktop
- [ ] fan oven
- [ ] fryer
- [ ] grill
- [ ] microwave
- [ ] static oven
- [ ]

Preservation — temp. / time
- [ ] freezer
- [ ] fridge
- [ ] room temp.
- [ ]

container
- [ ] airtight container
- [ ] cling film
- [ ] food-grade bag
- [ ]

Notes

Picture

Memo

Recipes used
- Vol.
- Vol.
- Vol.
- Vol.

Recipe's variants
- Vol.
- Vol.

Recipe

Difficulty 🎩🎩🎩🎩🎩　　Rating ☆☆☆☆☆　　📅 Date

author

🚩 **Nationality**　　📦 Dimensions　　⚖️ Weight　　🍪 Pieces　　👥 **Serves**

🧁 **Type** of dessert
- [ ] basic recipe
- [ ] cake
- [ ] chocolate
- [ ] cookie
- [ ] fried
- [ ] leavened
- [ ] pastry
- [ ] pie
- [ ] tart
- [ ]

🎉 **Ideal for**
- [ ] breakfast
- [ ] dessert
- [ ] snacks
- [ ] occasion
- [ ]

❄️ **Seasonal**
- [ ] spring
- [ ] summer
- [ ] fall
- [ ] winter
- [ ] year round

🍴 **Special diet**
- [ ] egg-free
- [ ] fat-free
- [ ] gluten-free
- [ ] lactose-free
- [ ] sugar-free
- [ ] vegan
- [ ] vegetarian
- [ ]

check ✓　🧂 **Ingredients**　⚖️ Quantity (Q)　Percentage (%=Q:Tx100)　🪙 Cost

🎂 **TOTAL** (Σ column values)　(T)　　100%

👥 **Per serving** (TOTAL : Serves)

🍴 **Utensils**
- ○ baking dish
- ○ baking paper
- ○ baking tin
- ○ baking tray
- ○ blender
- ○ bowl
- ○ cake scraper
- ○ chopping board
- ○ cling film
- ○ cookie cutter
- ○ cooking pan
- ○ cooling rack
- ○ cup
- ○ digital thermometer
- ○ dough mixer
- ○ electric whisk
- ○ fork
- ○ grater
- ○ kitchen scissors
- ○ kitchen torch
- ○ knife
- ○ ladle
- ○ measuring cups set
- ○ measuring spoons set
- ○ mixer
- ○ mold
- ○ offset spatula
- ○ pasta roller
- ○ pasta wheel
- ○ pastry brush
- ○ piping bag
- ○ piping nozzle
- ○ pot
- ○ potato peeler
- ○ revolving cake stand
- ○ rolling pin
- ○ rubber spatula
- ○ sieve
- ○ skimmer
- ○ soucepan
- ○ spoon
- ○ squeezer
- ○ strainer
- ○ teaspoon
- ○ weight scale
- ○ whisk
- ○
- ○
- ○
- ○

Instructions

Procedure / Time
- [ ] cooking
- [ ] cooling
- [ ] decorating
- [ ] freezing
- [ ] prepping
- [ ] proofing
- [ ] rest
- [ ]

TOT time

Cooking — temp. / time
- [ ] bain-marie
- [ ] cooktop
- [ ] fan oven
- [ ] fryer
- [ ] grill
- [ ] microwave
- [ ] static oven
- [ ]

Preservation — temp. / time
- [ ] freezer
- [ ] fridge
- [ ] room temp.
- [ ]

container
- [ ] airtight container
- [ ] cling film
- [ ] food-grade bag
- [ ]

Notes

Picture

Memo

Recipes used
- ◯ _____ Vol.
- ◯ _____ Vol.
- ◯ _____ Vol.
- ◯ _____ Vol.

Recipe's variants
- ◯ _____ Vol.
- ◯ _____ Vol.

Recipe

Difficulty ♗♗♗♗♗ Rating ☆☆☆☆☆ 📅 Date _____

_____ author _____

🚩 Nationality _____ 📺 Dimensions _____ ⚖ Weight _____ 🍪 Pieces _____ 👥 Serves _____

🧁 **Type** of dessert
- [ ] basic recipe
- [ ] cake
- [ ] chocolate
- [ ] cookie
- [ ] fried
- [ ] leavened
- [ ] pastry
- [ ] pie
- [ ] tart
- [ ]

🎉 **Ideal for**
- [ ] breakfast
- [ ] dessert
- [ ] snacks
- [ ] occasion
- [ ]

❄ **Seasonal**
- [ ] spring
- [ ] summer
- [ ] fall
- [ ] winter
- [ ] year round

🍴 **Special diet**
- [ ] egg-free
- [ ] fat-free
- [ ] gluten-free
- [ ] lactose-free
- [ ] sugar-free
- [ ] vegan
- [ ] vegetarian
- [ ]

check ✓

🥛 **Ingredients** | ⏲ Quantity (Q) | Percentage (%=Q:T×100) | 💰 Cost

🍰 **TOTAL** (Σ column values) _____ (T) _____ 100%
👥 **Per serving** (TOTAL : Serves) _____

🍴 **Utensils**
- ○ baking dish
- ○ baking paper
- ○ baking tin
- ○ baking tray
- ○ blender
- ○ bowl
- ○ cake scraper
- ○ chopping board
- ○ cling film
- ○ cookie cutter
- ○ cooking pan
- ○ cooling rack
- ○ cup
- ○ digital thermometer
- ○ dough mixer
- ○ electric whisk
- ○ fork
- ○ grater
- ○ kitchen scissors
- ○ kitchen torch
- ○ knife
- ○ ladle
- ○ measuring cups set
- ○ measuring spoons set
- ○ mixer
- ○ mold
- ○ offset spatula
- ○ pasta roller
- ○ pasta wheel
- ○ pastry brush
- ○ piping bag
- ○ piping nozzle
- ○ pot
- ○ potato peeler
- ○ revolving cake stand
- ○ rolling pin
- ○ rubber spatula
- ○ sieve
- ○ skimmer
- ○ soucepan
- ○ spoon
- ○ squeezer
- ○ strainer
- ○ teaspoon
- ○ weight scale
- ○ whisk
- ○
- ○

Instructions

Procedure | Time
- [ ] cooking
- [ ] cooling
- [ ] decorating
- [ ] freezing
- [ ] prepping
- [ ] proofing
- [ ] rest
- [ ]

TOT time

Cooking | temp. | time
- [ ] bain-marie
- [ ] cooktop
- [ ] fan oven
- [ ] fryer
- [ ] grill
- [ ] microwave
- [ ] static oven
- [ ]

Preservation | temp. | time
- [ ] freezer
- [ ] fridge
- [ ] room temp.
- [ ]

container
- [ ] airtight container
- [ ] cling film
- [ ] food-grade bag
- [ ]

Notes

Picture

Memo

Recipes used
- Vol.
- Vol.
- Vol.
- Vol.

Recipe's variants
- Vol.
- Vol.

Recipe

Difficulty ☺☺☺☺☺   Rating ☆☆☆☆☆   📅 Date

author

🚩 Nationality   📺 Dimensions   ⚖ Weight   🍪 Pieces   👥 Serves

🧁 Type of dessert
- ☐ basic recipe
- ☐ cake
- ☐ chocolate
- ☐ cookie
- ☐ fried
- ☐ leavened
- ☐ pastry
- ☐ pie
- ☐ tart
- ☐

🎉 Ideal for
- ☐ breakfast
- ☐ dessert
- ☐ snacks
- ☐ occasion
- ☐

❄ Seasonal
- ☐ spring
- ☐ summer
- ☐ fall
- ☐ winter
- ☐ year round

🍴 Special diet
- ☐ egg-free
- ☐ fat-free
- ☐ gluten-free
- ☐ lactose-free
- ☐ sugar-free
- ☐ vegan
- ☐ vegetarian
- ☐

check ✓ Ingredients   Quantity (Q)   Percentage (%=Q:T×100)   Cost

🎂 TOTAL (Σ column values)   (T)   100%

👥 Per serving (TOTAL : Serves)

🍴 Utensils
- ○ baking dish
- ○ baking paper
- ○ baking tin
- ○ baking tray
- ○ blender
- ○ bowl
- ○ cake scraper
- ○ chopping board
- ○ cling film
- ○ cookie cutter
- ○ cooking pan
- ○ cooling rack
- ○ cup
- ○ digital thermometer
- ○ dough mixer
- ○ electric whisk
- ○ fork
- ○ grater
- ○ kitchen scissors
- ○ kitchen torch
- ○ knife
- ○ ladle
- ○ measuring cups set
- ○ measuring spoons set
- ○ mixer
- ○ mold
- ○ offset spatula
- ○ pasta roller
- ○ pasta wheel
- ○ pastry brush
- ○ piping bag
- ○ piping nozzle
- ○ pot
- ○ potato peeler
- ○ revolving cake stand
- ○ rolling pin
- ○ rubber spatula
- ○ sieve
- ○ skimmer
- ○ soucepan
- ○ spoon
- ○ squeezer
- ○ strainer
- ○ teaspoon
- ○ weight scale
- ○ whisk
- ○
- ○
- ○
- ○

Instructions

Procedure / Time
- [ ] cooking
- [ ] cooling
- [ ] decorating
- [ ] freezing
- [ ] prepping
- [ ] proofing
- [ ] rest
- [ ]

TOT time

Cooking — temp. / time
- [ ] bain-marie
- [ ] cooktop
- [ ] fan oven
- [ ] fryer
- [ ] grill
- [ ] microwave
- [ ] static oven
- [ ]

Preservation — temp. / time
- [ ] freezer
- [ ] fridge
- [ ] room temp.
- [ ]

container
- [ ] airtight container
- [ ] cling film
- [ ] food-grade bag
- [ ]

Notes

Recipes used
- Vol.
- Vol.
- Vol.
- Vol.

Recipe's variants
- Vol.
- Vol.

Picture

Memo

Recipe

Difficulty ♟♟♟♟♟   Rating ☆☆☆☆☆   📅 Date _____

_____ author _____

🏁 Nationality _____   🎂 Dimensions _____   ⚖ Weight _____   🍪 Pieces _____   👥 Serves _____

🧁 Type of dessert
- ☐ basic recipe
- ☐ cake
- ☐ chocolate
- ☐ cookie
- ☐ fried
- ☐ leavened
- ☐ pastry
- ☐ pie
- ☐ tart
- ☐ _____

🎉 Ideal for
- ☐ breakfast
- ☐ dessert
- ☐ snacks
- ☐ occasion
- ☐ _____

❄ Seasonal
- ☐ spring
- ☐ summer
- ☐ fall
- ☐ winter
- ☐ year round

🍴 Special diet
- ☐ egg-free
- ☐ fat-free
- ☐ gluten-free
- ☐ lactose-free
- ☐ sugar-free
- ☐ vegan
- ☐ vegetarian
- ☐ _____

check ✓ | 🥫 Ingredients | ⚖ Quantity (Q) | Percentage (%=Q:T×100) | 🪙 Cost

(empty rows for ingredients)

🎂 **TOTAL** (Σ column values) _____ (T) _____ 100% _____

👥 **Per serving** (TOTAL : Serves) _____

🍴 Utensils

- ○ baking dish
- ○ baking paper
- ○ baking tin
- ○ baking tray
- ○ blender
- ○ bowl
- ○ cake scraper
- ○ chopping board
- ○ cling film
- ○ cookie cutter
- ○ cooking pan
- ○ cooling rack
- ○ cup
- ○ digital thermometer
- ○ dough mixer
- ○ electric whisk
- ○ fork
- ○ grater
- ○ kitchen scissors
- ○ kitchen torch
- ○ knife
- ○ ladle
- ○ measuring cups set
- ○ measuring spoons set
- ○ mixer
- ○ mold
- ○ offset spatula
- ○ pasta roller
- ○ pasta wheel
- ○ pastry brush
- ○ piping bag
- ○ piping nozzle
- ○ pot
- ○ potato peeler
- ○ revolving cake stand
- ○ rolling pin
- ○ rubber spatula
- ○ sieve
- ○ skimmer
- ○ soucepan
- ○ spoon
- ○ squeezer
- ○ strainer
- ○ teaspoon
- ○ weight scale
- ○ whisk
- ○ _____
- ○ _____
- ○ _____

Instructions

Procedure | Time
- [ ] cooking
- [ ] cooling
- [ ] decorating
- [ ] freezing
- [ ] prepping
- [ ] proofing
- [ ] rest
- [ ]

TOT time

Cooking | temp. | time
- [ ] bain-marie
- [ ] cooktop
- [ ] fan oven
- [ ] fryer
- [ ] grill
- [ ] microwave
- [ ] static oven
- [ ]

Preservation | temp. | time
- [ ] freezer
- [ ] fridge
- [ ] room temp.
- [ ]

container
- [ ] airtight container
- [ ] cling film
- [ ] food-grade bag
- [ ]

Notes

Picture

Memo

Recipes used
- Vol.
- Vol.
- Vol.
- Vol.

Recipe's variants
- Vol.
- Vol.

Recipe

Difficulty ☐☐☐☐☐ **Rating** ☆☆☆☆☆   📅 Date _____

_____   author _____

🚩 Nationality _____   📦 Dimensions ____   ⚖ Weight ____   🍪 Pieces ____   👥 **Serves** ____

🧁 Type of dessert
- ☐ basic recipe
- ☐ cake
- ☐ chocolate
- ☐ cookie
- ☐ fried
- ☐ leavened
- ☐ pastry
- ☐ pie
- ☐ tart
- ☐

🎉 Ideal for
- ☐ breakfast
- ☐ dessert
- ☐ snacks
- ☐ occasion
- ☐

❄ Seasonal
- ☐ spring
- ☐ summer
- ☐ fall
- ☐ winter
- ☐ year round

🍴 Special diet
- ☐ egg-free
- ☐ fat-free
- ☐ gluten-free
- ☐ lactose-free
- ☐ sugar-free
- ☐ vegan
- ☐ vegetarian
- ☐

check ✓ 🧂 Ingredients   ⏲ Quantity (Q)   Percentage (%=Q:T×100)   🪙 Cost

○ _____
○ _____
○ _____
○ _____
○ _____
○ _____
○ _____
○ _____
○ _____
○ _____
○ _____
○ _____
○ _____
○ _____
○ _____
○ _____
○ _____

🎂 **TOTAL** (Σ column values) _____ (T) _____   100%
👥 **Per serving** (TOTAL : Serves) _____

🍴 Utensils

○ baking dish	○ grater	○ revolving cake stand
○ baking paper	○ kitchen scissors	○ rolling pin
○ baking tin	○ kitchen torch	○ rubber spatula
○ baking tray	○ knife	○ sieve
○ blender	○ ladle	○ skimmer
○ bowl	○ measuring cups set	○ soucepan
○ cake scraper	○ measuring spoons set	○ spoon
○ chopping board	○ mixer	○ squeezer
○ cling film	○ mold	○ strainer
○ cookie cutter	○ offset spatula	○ teaspoon
○ cooking pan	○ pasta roller	○ weight scale
○ cooling rack	○ pasta wheel	○ whisk
○ cup	○ pastry brush	○
○ digital thermometer	○ piping bag	○
○ dough mixer	○ piping nozzle	○
○ electric whisk	○ pot	○
○ fork	○ potato peeler	○

Instructions

Procedure | Time
- [ ] cooking
- [ ] cooling
- [ ] decorating
- [ ] freezing
- [ ] prepping
- [ ] proofing
- [ ] rest
- [ ]

TOT time

Cooking | temp. | time
- [ ] bain-marie
- [ ] cooktop
- [ ] fan oven
- [ ] fryer
- [ ] grill
- [ ] microwave
- [ ] static oven
- [ ]

Preservation | temp. | time
- [ ] freezer
- [ ] fridge
- [ ] room temp.
- [ ]

container
- [ ] airtight container
- [ ] cling film
- [ ] food-grade bag
- [ ]

Notes

Recipes used
- Vol.
- Vol.
- Vol.
- Vol.

Recipe's variants
- Vol.
- Vol.

Picture

Memo

Recipe

Recipe Book

The end

Notes

Notes

Notes

Notes

3) Notes

Notes

Notes

Notes

Notes

Weights and Measures

Volume: Cups / Tablespoons / Teaspoons

CUP (C)

1C
8 fl.oz
240ml

TABLESPOON (TBPS)

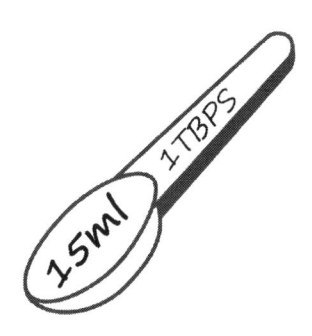

15ml / 1 TBPS

teaspoon (tsp)

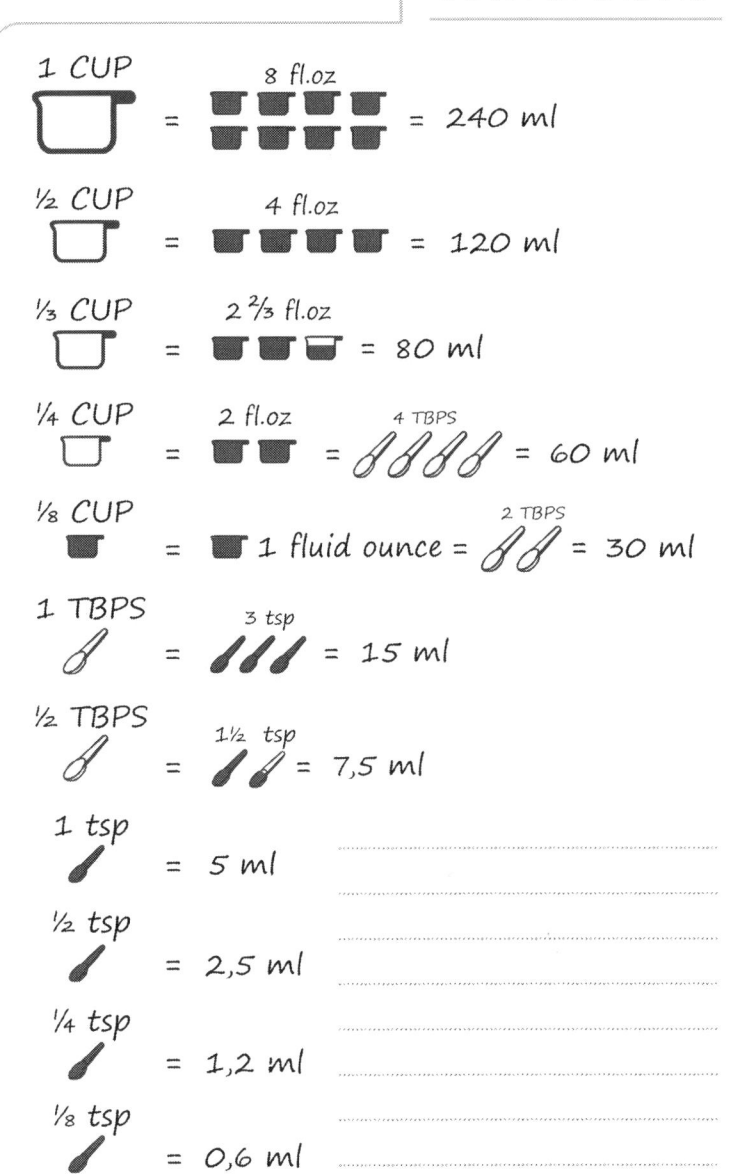

5ml / 1 tsp

CONVERSIONS

1 CUP = 8 fl.oz = 240 ml

½ CUP = 4 fl.oz = 120 ml

⅓ CUP = 2 ⅔ fl.oz = 80 ml

¼ CUP = 2 fl.oz = 4 TBPS = 60 ml

⅛ CUP = 1 fluid ounce = 2 TBPS = 30 ml

1 TBPS = 3 tsp = 15 ml

½ TBPS = 1½ tsp = 7,5 ml

1 tsp = 5 ml

½ tsp = 2,5 ml

¼ tsp = 1,2 ml

⅛ tsp = 0,6 ml

The measuring cups and spoons should leveled flat

Conversion table 1

Volume and Weights of ingredients

Ingredients

Leavening agents
	1C	1TBSP	1tsp
Backing soda		15 g	5 g
Backing powder		15 g	5 g
Active dry yest		10 g	3 g
Fresh yest		10 g	3 g

Starches and Flours
	1C	1TBSP	1tsp
Corn starch	140 g	9 g	3 g
Potato starch	140 g	9 g	3 g
Cake-Pastry flour	115 g	7 g	2 g
All-purpose flour	125 g	8 g	3 g
High gluten flour	140 g	9 g	3 g
Whole weat flour	120 g	7 g	2 g
Bread flour	130 g	8 g	3 g

Flavoring
	1C	1TBSP	1tsp
Cocoa powder	120 g	7 g	2 g
Vanilla extract		15 g	5 g
Salt		15 g	5 g

Fats/Oils/Butter
	1C	1TBSP	1tsp
Butter	230 g	15 g	5 g
Olive oil	215 g	13 g	4 g

Wet ingredients
	1C	1TBSP	1tsp
Water	240 g	15 g	5 g
Milk	245 g	15 g	5 g
Cream	245 g	15 g	5 g
Yogurt	245 g	15 g	5 g

Eggs (medium)
	1C	1TBSP	1tsp
Egg white	240 g	15 g	5 g
Egg yolk	300 g	19 g	7 g
Egg	275 g	17 g	6 g

Sugars
	1C	1TBSP	1tsp
Honey	340 g	20 g	7 g
Icing sugar	120 g	8 g	3 g
White sugar	200 g	12 g	4 g
Brown sugar	220 g	14 g	5 g

The measuring cups and spoons should leveled flat

Average weight of egg

- EGG SHELL 5g
- EGG YOLK 20g
- EGG WHITE 30g
- EGG 50g

2 Conversion table

Cake serving count and cutting guides

Cake pan Dimensions

Round (diameter)	Square (side)	Rectangular (side x side)
15 cm	13 cm	15x9 cm
18 cm	15 cm	20x10 cm
20 cm	18 cm	20x14 cm
23 cm	20 cm	25x15 cm
25 cm	23 cm	28x17 cm
28 cm	25 cm	30x20 cm
30 cm	28 cm	33x23 cm
35 cm	30 cm	38x25 cm
40 cm	35 cm	40x30 cm

Serves

Pies & Tarts	Layered Cakes
4	6-9
6	9-13
8	12-18
10	16-24
12	20-30
16	25-37
20	30-45
24	36-54
32	50-75

A serving of cake can weight 100-150g. The portions are subjective and vary depending on the type of cake, the height, the cut, the occasion, the appetite of the guests and so on. The values shown represent an estimate.

My serves

Cutting guides

Party cakes (5x5 cm)

Wedding cakes (3x5 cm)

Party cakes

Wedding cakes

Conversion table 3

Weight / Linear Measurements / Temperature

Weight

Imperial-Metric		Imperial-Metric	
⅛ oz	3,5 g	1lb 9oz	700 g
¼ oz	7 g	1lb 10oz	750 g
½ oz	15 g	1lb 12oz	800 g
¾ oz	20 g	1lb 14oz	850 g
1 oz	28 g	2 lb	900 g
1¼ oz	35 g	2lb 2oz	950 g
1½ oz	40 g	2lb 4oz	1 kg
1¾ oz	50 g	2lb 12oz	1,25 kg
2 oz	55 g	3 lb	1,35 kg
2¼ oz	65 g	3lb 5oz	1,5 kg
2½ oz	70 g	3lb 8oz	1,6 kg
2¾ oz	80 g	4 lb	1,8 kg
3 oz	85 g	4lb 8oz	2 kg
3¼ oz	90 g	5 lb	2,25 kg
3½ oz	100 g	5lb 8oz	2,5 kg
4 oz	115 g	6 lb	2,7 kg
4½ oz	125 g	6lb 8oz	3 kg
5 oz	140 g		
5½ oz	155 g		
6 oz	170 g		
6½ oz	185 g		
7 oz	200 g		
7½ oz	215 g		
8 oz	225 g		
8½ oz	240 g		
9 oz	255 g		
9½ oz	270 g		
10 oz	280 g		
10½ oz	300 g		
11 oz	315 g		
11½ oz	325 g		
12 oz	340 g		
12½ oz	355 g		
13 oz	370 g		
13½ oz	385 g		
14 oz	400 g		
14½ oz	410 g		
15 oz	425 g		
1 lb	450 g		
1lb 2oz	500 g		
1lb 3oz	550 g		
1lb 5oz	600 g		
1lb 7oz	650 g		

Linear Measurements

Imperial-Metric		Imperial-Metric	
⅛ in	3 mm	10¼ in	26 cm
¼ in	6 mm	10¾ in	27 cm
⅜ in	1 mm	11 in	28 cm
½ in	1,3 cm	11½ in	29 cm
⅝ in	1,5 cm	12 in	30 cm
¾ in	2 cm	12¼ in	31 cm
1 in	2,5 cm	12½ in	32 cm
1¼ in	3 cm	13 in	33 cm
1½ in	4 cm	13½ in	34 cm
1¾ in	4,5 cm	14 in	35 cm
2 in	5 cm	14¼ in	36 cm
2¼ in	5,5 cm	14½ in	37 cm
2½ in	6 cm	15 in	38 cm
2¾ in	7 cm	15½ in	39 cm
3 in	7,5 cm	15¾ in	40 cm
3¼ in	8 cm	16 in	41 cm
3½ in	9 cm	16½ in	42 cm
3¾ in	9,5 cm	17 in	43 cm
4 in	10 cm	17½ in	44 cm
4¼ in	11 cm	17¾ in	45 cm
4½ in	11,5 cm	18 in	46 cm
4¾ in	12 cm	18½ in	47 cm
5 in	13 cm	19 in	48 cm
5¼ in	13,5 cm	19½ in	49 cm
5½ in	14 cm	20 in	50 cm
5¾ in	14,5 cm		
6 in	15 cm		
6¼ in	16 cm		
6½ in	16,5 cm		
6¾ in	17 cm		
7 in	18 cm		
7¼ in	18,5 cm		
7½ in	19 cm		
7¾ in	19,5 cm		
8 in	20 cm		
8¼ in	21 cm		
8½ in	21,5 cm		
8¾ in	22 cm		
9 in	23 cm		
9¼ in	23,5 cm		
9½ in	24 cm		
9¾ in	25 cm		
10 in	25,5 cm		

Temperature

Fahrenheit-Celsius

225°F = 110°C
250°F = 120°C
275°F = 135°C
300°F = 150°C
325°F = 165°F
350°F = 180°C
375°F = 190°C
400°F = 200°C
425°F = 220°C
450°F = 230°C

Conversion table

Bookmarks

Make your own bookmarks!

Cut out the squares along the dark lines and following the folding instructions below.

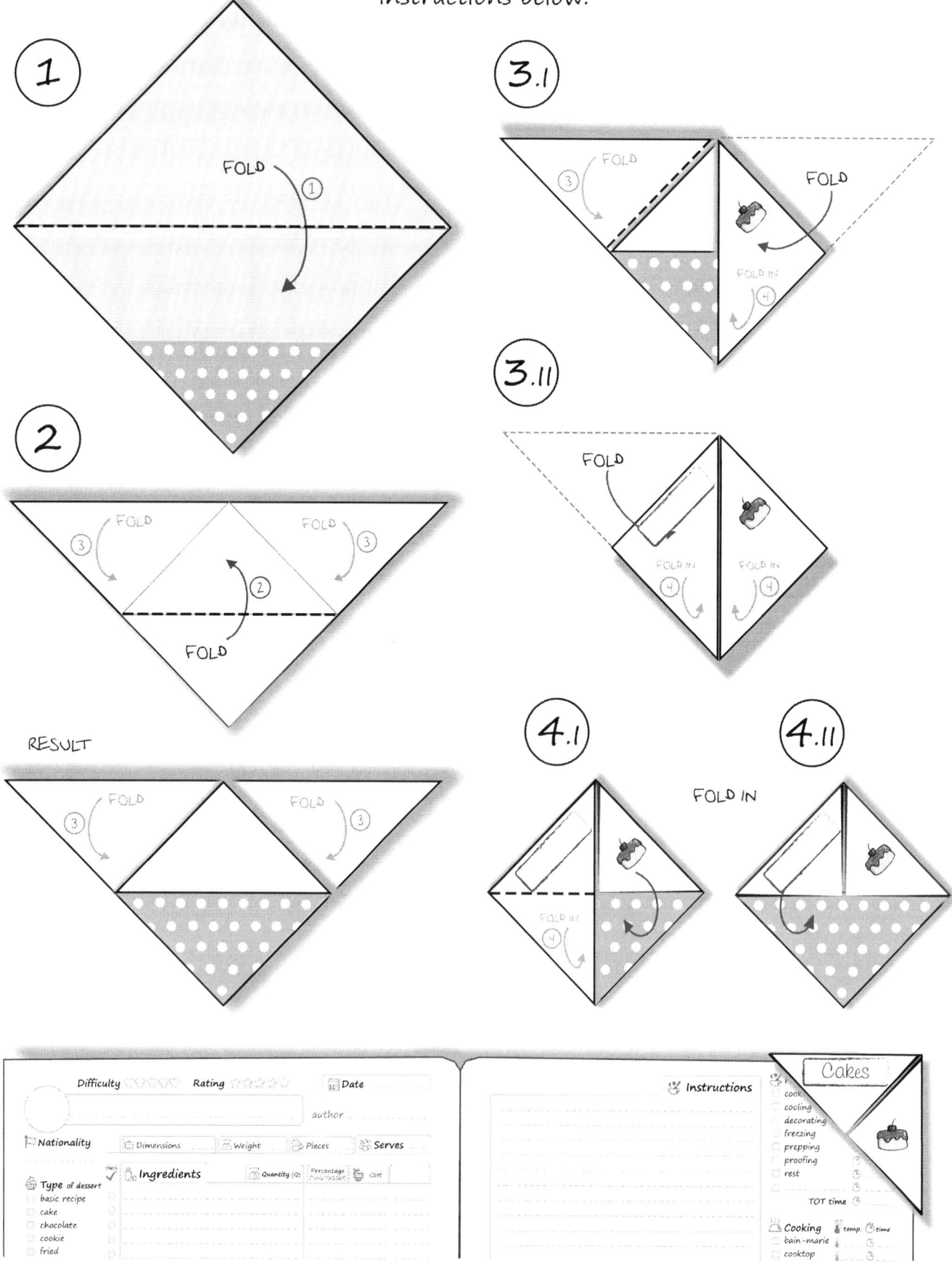

FOLD

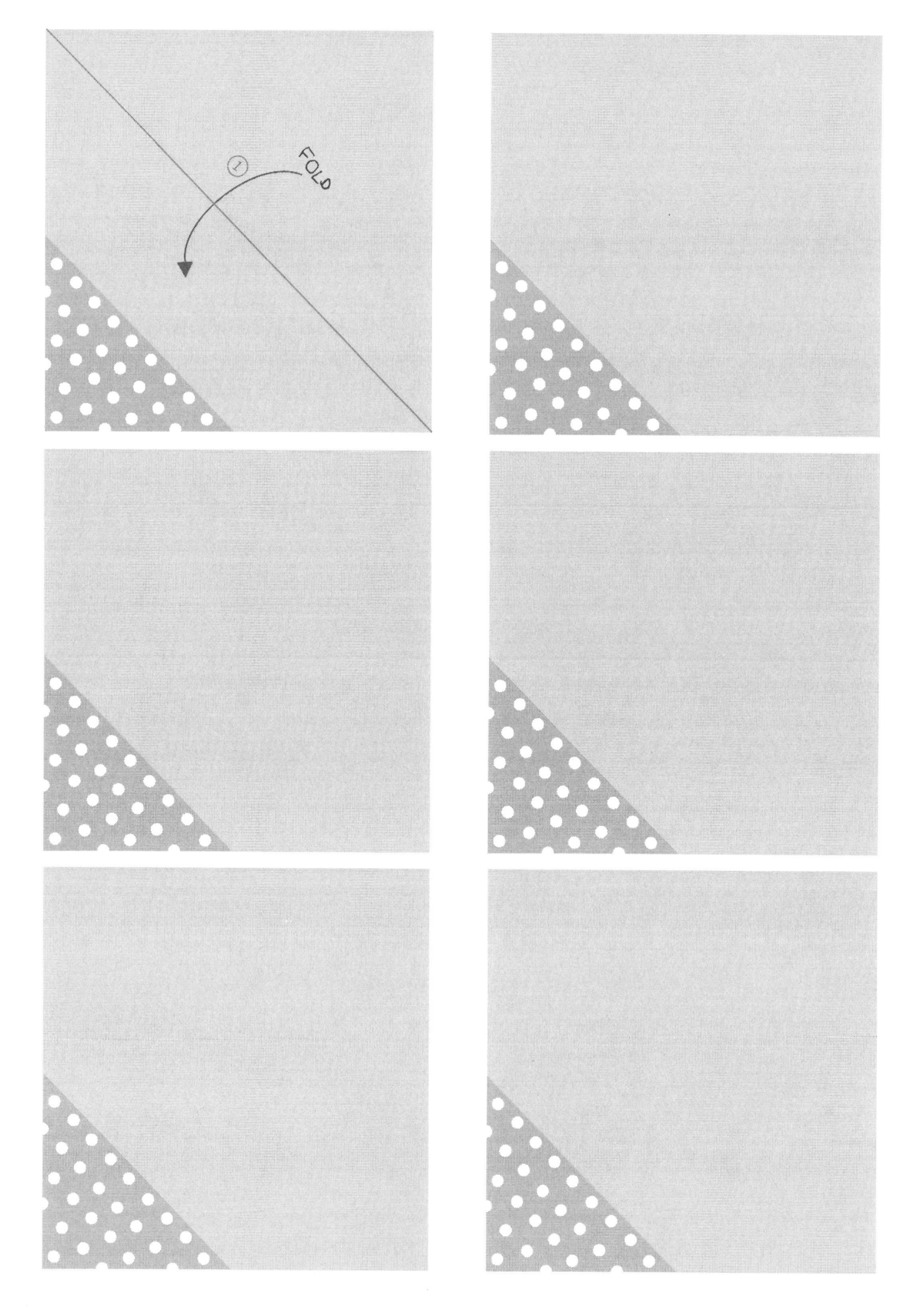

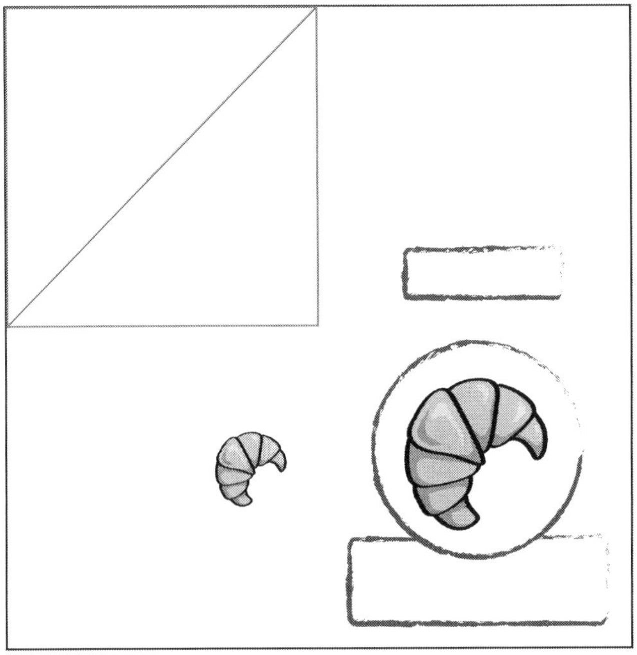

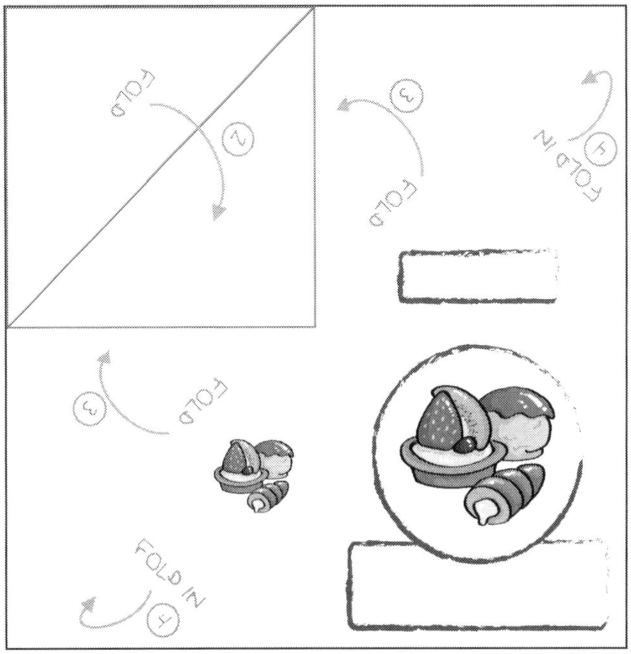
FOLD
FOLD
FOLD IN
FOLD
FOLD IN

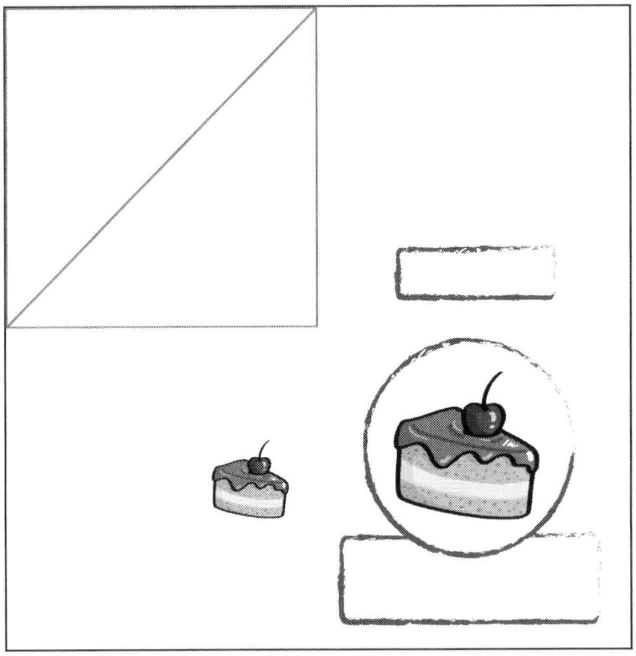

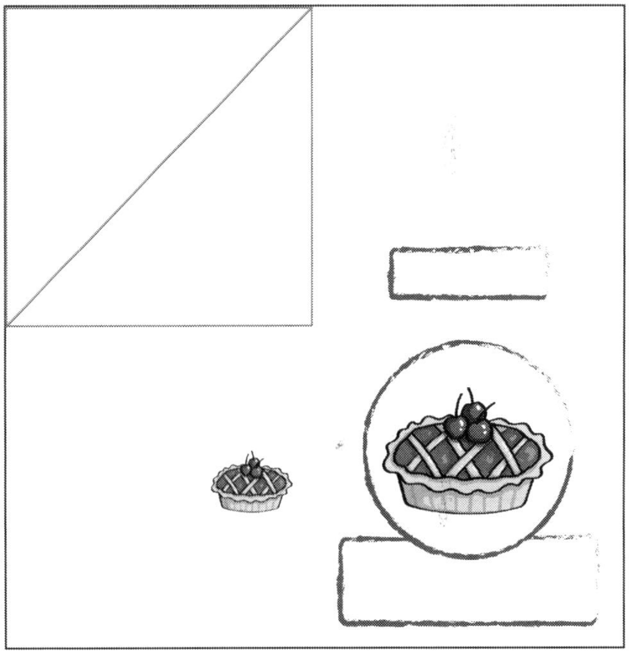

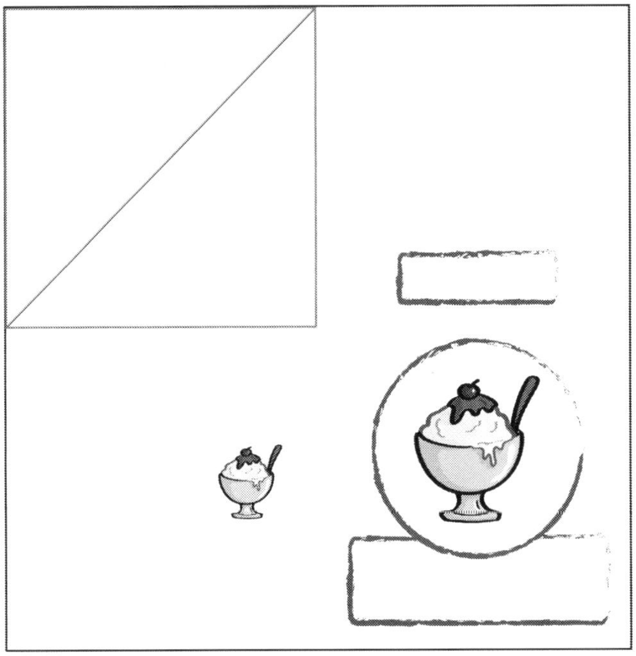

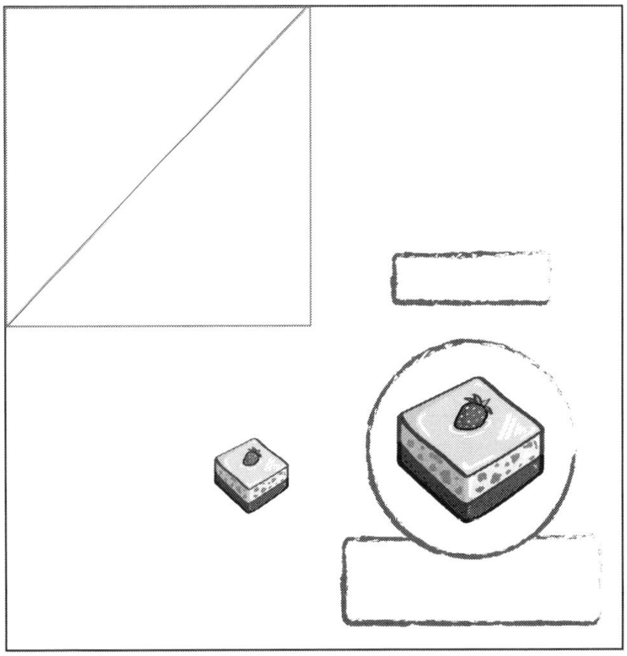

FOLD

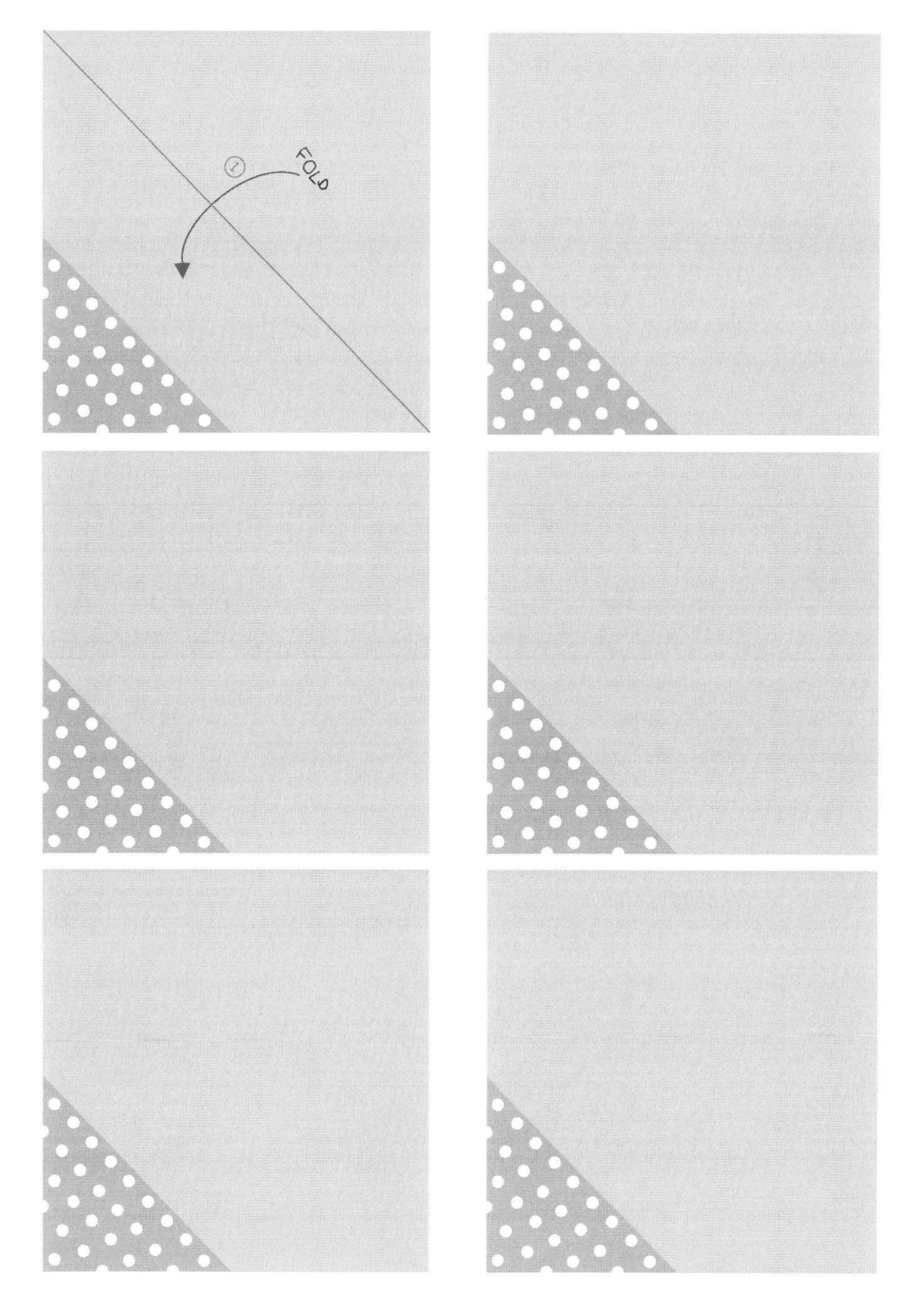

il mondo di ielle
sugar Art
www.ilmondodiielle.com

Printed in Great
Britain
by Amazon